State Exam Review for Cosmetology

Delmar Publishers' Online Services

To access Delmar on the World Wide Web, point your browser to:

http://www.delmar.com/delmar.html

To access through Gopher: gopher://gopher.delmar.com

(Delmar Online is part of "thomson.com", an Internet site with information on
more than 30 publishers of the International Thomson Publishing organization.)

For information on our products and services:

email: info@delmar.com

or call 800-347-7707

State Exam Review for Cosmetology

Milady Publishing Company

Typical State Board Examination Questions

Follows closely the National Testing and State Board Requirements

By Milady Staff

edited by Linnea M. Lindquist, Minneapolis Technical College

ISBN 1-56253-237-5

© Copyright 1957, 1962, 1965, 1968, 1969, 1971, 1981, 1982, 1985, 1988, 1989, 1991, 1995

Milady Publishing Company
(A Division of Delmar Publishers Inc.)

Library of Congress Catalog Card Number: 93-26375

Printed in the United States of America

Printed and distributed simultaneously in Canada

Milady Publishing Company
(A Division of Delmar Publishers Inc.)
3 Columbia Circle, Box 12519
Albany, NY 12212

5 6 7 8 9 10 XXX 01 00 99 98 97 96

FOREWORD

The State Exam Review for Cosmetology has been revised to follow very closely the type of cosmetology questions most frequently used by states and by the national testing, conducted under the auspices of the National-Interstate Council of State Boards of Cosmetology.

This review book is designed to be of major assistance to students in preparing for the state license examinations. In addition, its regular use in the classroom will serve as an important aid in the understanding of all subjects taught in cosmetology schools and required in the practice of cosmetology.

The exclusive concentration on multiple choice test items is due to the fact that all state board examinations and national testing examinations are confined to this type of question.

Students who diligently study and practice their work as taught in the classroom and who use this book for test preparation and review should receive higher grades on both classroom and license examinations.

THE AUTHORS

CONTENTS

Your Professional Image

1. The science that deals with healthful living is:
   a) chemistry
   b) hygiene
   c) bacteriology
   d) cosmetology ____

2. The science that deals with the daily maintenance of health by the individual is:
   a) good grooming
   b) self-preservation
   c) personal hygiene
   d) personal development ____

3. Personal hygiene deals with the preservation of the well-being of the:
   a) individual
   b) community
   c) town
   d) society ____

4. The practice of public sanitation is important because it helps to preserve the:
   a) quality of cosmetology services
   b) health of the individual
   c) health of the community
   d) quality of cosmetology products ____

5. Public hygiene is also known as:
   a) personal hygiene
   b) sterilization
   c) sanitation
   d) disinfection ____

6. Exercise helps to stimulate:
   a) bad breath
   b) malnutrition
   c) blood circulation
   d) cleanliness ____

7. The body may be kept clean by the regular use of:
   a) deodorants
   b) soap and water
   c) disinfectants
   d) germicides ____

8. Body odors can be prevented by regular bathing and use of:
   a) styptics
   b) astringents
   c) vapors
   d) deodorants ____

9. Maintaining healthy teeth and keeping the breath sweet is known as:
   a) facial sterilization
   b) oral hygiene
   c) mouth deodorization
   d) mouth lubrication ____

10. To keep your teeth in a good, healthy condition, it is necessary to maintain regular:
    a) use of disinfectants
    b) oral exercise
    c) use of deodorants
    d) dental care ____

11. Bad or offensive breath may be treated and minimized by:
    a) gargling with an astringent
    b) spraying with a disinfectant
    c) spraying with a perfumed caustic
    d) rinsing with mouthwash ____

12. Rest and relaxation are necessary to prevent:
    a) fatigue
    b) poor eating habits
    c) poor oral hygiene
    d) body odors   _____

13. Overexertion and lack of rest tend to drain the body of its:
    a) nervous system
    b) efficiency
    c) body odors
    d) blood supply   _____

14. The psychology of getting along with others is called:
    a) physical presentation
    b) human relations
    c) good posture
    d) public hygiene   _____

15. One of the major elements required for good health is:
    a) a well-balanced diet
    b) freedom from cavities
    c) styptic formation
    d) personal disinfection   _____

16. Factors that may be considered health hazards are:
    a) moderate work and play
    b) impure air and food
    c) clean body and clothes
    d) efficient salon practices   _____

17. One of the best advertisements of an effectively run beauty salon is a cosmetologist who is:
    a) well groomed
    b) disheveled
    c) fatigued
    d) nervous and worried   _____

18. Courage, hope, and cheerfulness are three mental qualities necessary for good:
    a) sanitation
    b) fatigue
    c) health
    d) oxidation   _____

19. An important consideration in personal hygiene is:
    a) personal emotion
    b) efficiency
    c) ethical conduct
    d) cleanliness   _____

20. Two emotions that can be injurious to good health are worry and:
    a) hope
    b) courage
    c) fear
    d) sincerity   _____

21. To be successful, it is most important to avoid body odor and:
    a) courtesy
    b) punctuality
    c) bad breath
    d) good grooming   _____

22. The cosmetologist who practices correct posture will find that it helps to reduce:
    a) skin discoloration
    b) body fatigue
    c) dandruff
    d) muscular coordination   _____

23. For a good standing posture, keep the head up, chin level with floor, chest up, shoulders relaxed, and:
    a) lower abdomen out
    b) knees close together
    c) lower abdomen flat
    d) feet wide apart   _____

24. For a good sitting posture, keep the feet and:
    a) arms close together
    b) knees close together
    c) chin out
    d) chest relaxed   _____

25. For a comfortable sitting posture, keep the soles of the feet:
    a) on the floor
    b) crossed
    c) extended
    d) elevated ____

26. The muscles of the body are kept in good condition by:
    a) tonics
    b) caustics
    c) conditioners
    d) exercise ____

27. In order to give the body support and balance and to help maintain good posture, the cosmetologist should wear:
    a) a uniform
    b) high-heeled shoes
    c) low-heeled shoes
    d) house slippers ____

28. Personal hygiene includes all of the following EXCEPT:
    a) brushing your teeth
    b) bathing or showering
    c) cleansing your nails
    d) wearing the latest fashions ____

29. To avoid back strain while working, sit:
    a) toward the back of the chair
    b) in a slouching position
    c) on the forward part of the chair
    d) rigidly upright ____

30. The minimizing of fatigue is one of the benefits of maintaining good:
    a) personality
    b) posture
    c) hygiene
    d) appearance ____

31. To avoid back strain while giving a shampoo or other beauty service, maintain a:
    a) sway-back posture
    b) lordosis posture
    c) good posture
    d) kyphosis posture ____

32. Skills that include listening, manners of speaking, and your voice are all a part of:
    a) physical presentation
    b) human relations
    c) communication
    d) professional attitude ____

33. Rules involving professional ethics for cosmetology include all of the following EXCEPT:
    a) respecting other's beliefs and rights
    b) being loyal to your employer/manager and coworkers
    c) treating everyone honestly and fairly
    d) getting adequate rest and nutrition ____

34. The outward reflection of a person's inner feelings is called:
    a) personal vitality
    b) personality
    c) good grooming
    d) courtesy ____

35. It will be helpful to a student's success to develop a/an:
    a) list of good stories
    b) arrogant attitude
    c) crisp, business-only attitude
    d) pleasing personality ____

36. A very important attribute of a pleasing personality is a good:
   a) financial standing
   b) list of stories
   c) loud voice
   d) sense of humor ____

37. Thoughtfulness of others is considered to be the foundation of:
   a) good grooming
   b) personality development
   c) vitality
   d) courtesy ____

38. The use of good speech is vital to the art of:
   a) literature
   b) fashion
   c) conversation
   d) grooming ____

39. Good topics for salon conversation should be:
   a) political
   b) debatable
   c) religious
   d) noncontroversial ____

40. A smile of greeting and a word of welcome are two personality characteristics that reflect:
   a) liveliness
   b) graciousness
   c) good education
   d) sense of humor ____

41. Courtesy is the key to:
   a) failure
   b) success
   c) good looks
   d) outsmarting others ____

42. One of the cosmetologist's most important personal assets is his/her:
   a) loud voice
   b) personality
   c) clothes
   d) arrogance ____

43. It is advisable that the cosmetologist develop a:
   a) sense of humor
   b) crisp attitude
   c) list of good jokes
   d) popularity status ____

44. The cosmetologist should try to fit the conversation to the client's:
   a) sex life
   b) religion
   c) politics
   d) mood ____

45. Good conversation involves the use of a pleasant voice, good choice of words, intelligence, charm, and:
   a) grooming
   b) impatience
   c) personality
   d) profanity ____

46. Proper conduct in relation to employer, clients, and coworkers is called professional:
   a) personality
   b) ethics
   c) courtesy
   d) honesty ____

47. Repeating gossip will cause loss of the patron's:
   a) attention
   b) charm
   c) confidence
   d) posture ____

48. An important attribute of good professional ethics is:
   a) bad temper
   b) loyalty
   c) arrogance
   d) gossip ____

49. One important ingredient of a proper professional attitude is:
    a) arrogance
    c) punctuality
    b) posture
    d) antecedents ____

50. All clients must be treated honestly and fairly, without any demonstration of:
    a) confidence
    c) dignity
    b) courtesy
    d) favoritism ____

51. Clients will respect and be loyal to a cosmetologist who is:
    a) arrogant
    c) temperamental
    b) illiterate
    d) courteous ____

52. The true professional treats the feelings and rights of others with:
    a) disdain
    c) respect
    b) severity
    d) arrogance ____

53. The wise and successful cosmetologist is most often a good:
    a) storyteller
    c) listener
    b) gossiper
    d) babbler ____

54. Clients should always be addressed by their:
    a) nicknames
    c) eye color
    b) hair color
    d) names ____

55. To be liked, it is important to handle clients with:
    a) profanity
    c) disdain
    b) tact
    d) arrogance ____

56. Client's complaints and grievances should be treated promptly and:
    a) judiciously
    c) roughly
    b) unfairly
    d) arrogantly ____

Bacteriology

1. The scientific study of microorganisms is known as:
   a) pathology
   b) biology
   c) bacteriology
   d) genealogy ____

2. Bacteria are one-celled microorganisms of:
   a) animal origin
   b) vegetable origin
   c) mineral origin
   d) chemical origin ____

3. Pathogenic bacteria are commonly found:
   a) on a clean body
   b) on sterile implements
   c) in dirty places
   d) on clean towels ____

4. Pathogenic bacteria produce:
   a) health
   b) disease
   c) antitoxins
   d) beneficial effects ____

5. Harmful bacteria are referred to as:
   a) saprophytes
   b) pathogenic
   c) nonpathogenic
   d) protozoa ____

6. Nonpathogenic bacteria are:
   a) harmful
   b) cocci
   c) harmless
   d) disease producing ____

7. Pathogenic bacteria are commonly known as:
   a) antiseptics
   b) disinfectants
   c) germs
   d) beneficial bacteria ____

8. Bacteria are best seen by using:
   a) a microscope
   b) a telescope
   c) regular eyeglasses
   d) sunglasses ____

9. Cocci are bacteria with a:
   a) round shape
   b) rod shape
   c) corkscrew shape
   d) curved shape ____

10. Bacilli are bacteria with a:
    a) corkscrew shape
    b) round shape
    c) rod shape
    d) curved shape ____

11. Spirilla are bacteria with a:
    a) round shape
    b) corkscrew shape
    c) rod shape
    d) flat shape ____

12. Bacteria cells reproduce by simply dividing in:
    a) half
    b) quarters
    c) thirds
    d) eighths ____

13. Pustules and boils are infections containing:
    a) nonpathogenic organisms
    b) pathogenic bacteria
    c) sebum
    d) ringworm ____

14. Bacteria are also known as germs or:
    - a) viruses
    - b) fungi
    - c) microbes
    - d) verrucae

15. Some forms of bacteria have the ability to move about with the aid of:
    - a) flagella
    - b) spores
    - c) viruses
    - d) none of the above ____

16. The inactive phase in the life cycle of bacteria is known as the:
    - a) pathogenic stage
    - b) spore-forming stage
    - c) disease-producing stage
    - d) nonpathogenic stage ____

17. A communicable disease is:
    - a) not transferred from one person to another
    - b) not responsible for an epidemic
    - c) transmitted from one person to another
    - d) caused by nonpathogenic bacteria ____

18. Disease may be spread in a beauty salon by:
    - a) clean hands
    - b) unclean hands
    - c) clean towels
    - d) sanitized implements ____

19. A boil is an example of:
    - a) a general infection
    - b) a local infection
    - c) nonpathogenic bacteria
    - d) a noncontagious disease ____

20. Bacteria may enter the body through:
    - a) dry skin
    - b) moist skin
    - c) broken skin
    - d) oily skin ____

21. Resistance to disease is known as:
    - a) infection
    - b) immunity
    - c) a parasite
    - d) a fungus ____

22. An example of a general infection is:
    - a) a boil
    - b) syphilis
    - c) a verruca
    - d) a skin lesion ____

23. Organisms that live on other organisms without giving anything in return are known as:
    - a) favus
    - b) canities
    - c) diphtheria
    - d) parasites ____

24. Cosmetologists should not work on patrons if they have a:
    - a) common cold
    - b) carbuncle
    - c) keratoma
    - d) verruca ____

25. AIDS is the abbreviation for:
    - a) All In Debt Salon
    - b) plastic gloves
    - c) Acquired Immune Deficiency Syndrome
    - d) the bank ____

26. AIDS is caused by:
    - a) the HIV virus
    - b) listening to loud music
    - c) lack of proper nutrition
    - d) the flu ____

27. AIDS may be transferred in the salon by:
    a) sharing snacks
    b) using the telephone
    c) shampooing too long
    d) using unsanitized
       implements   ____

Decontamination and Infection Control

1. A clean salon promotes clients':
   a) germs
   b) color
   c) confidence
   d) retail purchases _____

2. Federal and state regulations require salons to protect against:
   a) lawsuits
   b) spread of germs
   c) chapped hands
   d) poor coffee _____

3. Injury and illness in salons is caused by:
   a) carelessness
   b) bad products
   c) training sessions
   d) bad breath _____

4. Removing pathogens and other substances from tools or surfaces is called:
   a) cleaning
   b) autoclaving
   c) scrubbing
   d) decontamination _____

5. A level of decontamination not practical for salons is:
   a) mold
   b) sterilization
   c) clean air
   d) sanitary _____

6. Surfaces in a salon are sanitized by washing with:
   a) alcohol
   b) baby shampoo
   c) soap
   d) distilled water _____

7. Washing your hands with liquid soap and water is an example of:
   a) sanitation
   b) preparing for lunch
   c) good manners
   d) sterilization _____

8. An antiseptic is a safe solution to use for sanitizing:
   a) bleached hair
   b) skin
   c) permed hair
   d) salon floor _____

9. Killing microbes on contaminated tools and other surfaces requires use of a:
   a) microphone
   b) cold water
   c) dust mop
   d) disinfectant _____

10. A disinfectant should never be used on:
    a) floors
    b) bathroom fixtures
    c) human skin, hair, or nails
    d) manicure implements _____

11. The federal government agency that must approve disinfectants for use is the:
    a) SPCA
    b) EPA
    c) OSHA
    d) NIH _____

12. To prevent accidental exposure when working with disinfectants you should wear:
    a) gloves
    b) thongs
    c) light-colored clothing
    d) dark-colored clothing _____

13. OSHA stands for:
    a) Outside Happiness
    b) a brand of bleach
    c) Occupational Safety and Health Administration
    d) Other Society for Halloween ____

14. Product content is information that should be listed on a/an:
    a) MSDS
    b) tax return
    c) OSHA form
    d) inventory sheet ____

15. A hospital-level disinfectant will kill harmful bacteria and destroy:
    a) cigarette smoke
    b) fungus
    c) split ends
    d) soap ____

16. Before soaking in a disinfecting solutions, all implements should be thoroughly:
    a) used
    b) wet
    c) cleaned
    d) covered in soap ____

17. A container used to hold disinfecting solution and soak implements is called a/an:
    a) implement jar
    b) wet sanitizer
    c) soaking bottle
    d) water bottle ____

18. To avoid spreading pathogens, never touch a client's:
    a) head
    b) hand
    c) back
    d) open sore or wound ____

19. Sodium hypochlorite is the chemical name for:
    a) shampoos
    b) conditioners
    c) household bleach
    d) water softeners ____

20. 99% isopropyl alcohol equals the same strength as ____ ethyl alcohol.
    a) 50%
    b) 70%
    c) 65%
    d) 45% ____

21. Quaternary ammonium compounds disinfect implements in:
    a) 10 to 15 minutes
    b) 30 minutes
    c) 5 minutes or less
    d) 20 minutes ____

22. A disinfectant that can corrode tools and dull sharp edges is:
    a) hand wipes
    b) aerosol
    c) alcohol
    d) too strong ____

23. A safe and fast-acting disinfectant is:
    a) Pepto-Bismol
    b) quats
    c) air fresheners
    d) corrosive ____

24. An ultrasonic bath cleans by creating:
    a) loud booms
    b) a mess
    c) soft water
    d) high-frequency sound waves ____

25. Ultrasonic baths are good for cleaning implements':
    a) disposable parts
    b) over 2 weeks old
    c) nooks and crannies
    d) that must stay dry ____

26. An ultrasonic bath is only effective when used with a/an:
    a) disinfectant
    b) bubble bath
    c) autoclave
    d) assistant to operate
    _____

27. Disinfectants should be stored in containers that have been:
    a) sterilized
    b) labeled
    c) recycled
    d) opened
    _____

28. A disinfectant no longer considered safe for salon use is:
    a) Lysol
    b) soap
    c) formalin
    d) hot water
    _____

29. Hand soap in a salon should be this type:
    a) moisturizing
    b) cheap
    c) bar
    d) pump-type liquid antiseptic
    _____

30. Before a surface is disinfected, it should be:
    a) dirty
    b) cleaned
    c) replaced
    d) laminated
    _____

31. To disinfect surfaces, disinfectant must be left on for at least:
    a) 5 minutes
    b) 30 minutes
    c) 10 minutes
    d) overnight
    _____

32. A properly disinfected surface has disinfectant applied _____ times during the procedure.
    a) two
    b) four
    c) three
    d) five
    _____

33. The final step in disinfecting a surface is:
    a) blow-drying
    b) wipe with chamois
    c) air drying
    d) wipe with paper towel
    _____

34. Properly disinfected tools should be stored in a:
    a) pocket
    b) wet sanitizer
    c) towel
    d) sealed, airtight container
    _____

35. An inexpensive way to store disinfected tools is to wrap in:
    a) clean plastic wrap
    b) washcloths
    c) paper towels
    d) waxed paper
    _____

Properties of the Hair and Scalp

1. Hair is an outgrowth on the:
   a) palms
   b) soles
   c) scalp and skin
   d) lips   ____

2. The primary purpose of hair is to:
   a) keep the scalp oily
   b) protect and adorn
   c) keep the scalp dry
   d) keep dandruff in place   ____

3. Hair is chiefly composed of a substance called:
   a) hemoglobin
   b) melanin
   c) keratin
   d) calcium   ____

4. No sense of feeling is found in the:
   a) skin
   b) hair
   c) fingers
   d) lips   ____

5. The hair takes its shape, size, and direction from its:
   a) cortex
   b) cuticle
   c) medulla
   d) follicle   ____

6. A cross-sectional view of wavy hair reveals a/an:
   a) round shape
   b) flat shape
   c) oval shape
   d) square shape   ____

7. A cross-sectional view of curly hair reveals almost a:
   a) flat shape
   b) round shape
   c) wavy shape
   d) square shape   ____

8. A cross-sectional view of straight hair reveals a/an:
   a) square shape
   b) oval shape
   c) round shape
   d) flat shape   ____

9. The hair root is that portion of the hair contained within the:
   a) hair cuticle
   b) hair follicle
   c) sweat pore
   d) hair cortex   ____

10. The lower part of the hair bulb is hollowed to fit over the:
    a) root
    b) follicle
    c) papilla
    d) shaft   ____

11. The club-shaped structure forming the lower part of the hair root is called the hair:
    a) bulb
    b) shaft
    c) follicle
    d) papilla   ____

12. Hair growth starts in the hair:
    a) shaft
    b) bulb
    c) root
    d) papilla   ____

13. The hair follicle is a tubelike pocket that:
    a) encircles the cuticle
    b) encircles the medulla
    c) extends beyond the skin
    d) encases, or encloses the hair root   ____

14. At the bottom of the hair follicle is found a small cone-shaped elevation called the hair:
    a) papilla
    b) cuticle
    c) medulla
    d) cortex
    ____

15. Hair receives its nourishment from the hair papilla, which contains:
    a) blood vessels
    b) muscles
    c) glands
    d) fatty tissue
    ____

16. The medulla of the hair is found in the:
    a) center of the hair
    b) outer layer of hair
    c) second layer of hair
    d) cuticle layer of hair
    ____

17. The hair cuticle is the:
    a) center layer
    b) outer layer
    c) second layer
    d) marrow
    ____

18. The hair cortex is the:
    a) outer layer
    b) center layer
    c) inner (second) layer
    d) marrow
    ____

19. Hair strength and elasticity are from the hair:
    a) medulla
    b) cuticle
    c) follicle
    d) cortex
    ____

20. Coloring matter is found in the hair:
    a) bulb
    b) cuticle
    c) cortex
    d) follicle
    ____

21. Hair pigment is derived from color-forming substances in the:
    a) heart
    b) liver
    c) blood
    d) spleen
    ____

22. When the pigment is gone and air spaces develop, the hair appears to be:
    a) black
    b) brown
    c) red
    d) gray
    ____

23. A person with no coloring matter in his/her hair is a/an:
    a) brunette
    b) brownette
    c) albino
    d) redhead
    ____

24. The muscle connected to the hair follicle is called the:
    a) epicranius
    b) arrector pili
    c) procerus
    d) auricularis
    ____

25. Dry normal hair can stretch to about:
    a) ½ its natural length
    b) ⅕ its natural length
    c) ¾ its natural length
    d) double its natural length
    ____

26. The arrector pili is a muscle responsible for:
    a) hair texture
    b) hair porosity
    c) goose bumps
    d) hair elasticity
    ____

27. No hair is found on the:
    a) skin
    b) lips
    c) scalp
    d) chin
    ____

28. The average life of hair on the head is about:
    a) 8–10 months
    b) 12–15 months
    c) 4–7 years
    d) more than 8 years
    ____

29. On the eyebrows and eyelashes are found:
    a) lanugo hair
    b) long hair
    c) short, bristly hair
    d) downy hair
    ____

30. Hypertrichosis means the growth on the body of excess:
    a) hair
    b) skin
    c) warts
    d) keratoma
    ____

31. Eyelashes and eyebrows are replaced approximately every:
    a) other month
    b) 2 months
    c) 8–9 months
    d) 4–5 months
    ____

32. The sebaceous glands supply sebum that keeps the hair:
    a) dull
    b) soft
    c) coarse
    d) long
    ____

33. The average rate of hair growth on the head is about:
    a) ¼" a month
    b) ½" a month
    c) ¼" a week
    d) ½" a week
    ____

34. The natural color of hair and its strength and texture mainly depend on:
    a) the hair stream
    b) cowlicks
    c) heredity
    d) hirsuties
    ____

35. If the papilla is destroyed, the hair will:
    a) grow again
    b) grow longer
    c) grow shorter
    d) never grow again
    ____

36. The texture refers to the degree of the hair's:
    a) softness or hardness
    b) coarseness or fineness
    c) elasticity
    d) medulla
    ____

37. A hard, glassy finish is characteristic of hair texture that is:
    a) fine
    b) short
    c) medium
    d) wiry
    ____

38. Porosity is the ability of the hair to absorb:
    a) keratin
    b) sunshine
    c) moisture
    d) ultraviolet rays
    ____

39. A small piece of hair standing up is known as a/an:
    a) cowlick
    b) arrector
    c) crown
    d) albino
    ____

40. Hair elasticity is the ability of the hair to:
    a) accept tints
    b) absorb moisture, expand, and stretch
    c) stretch and break
    d) stretch and return to its original shape without breaking ____

41. The direction of the natural flow of hair on the scalp is known as hair:
    a) whorl
    b) stream
    c) arch
    d) cowlick ____

42. The coloring matter of the hair is called:
    a) keratin
    b) hematocyte
    c) melanin
    d) aniline ____

43. Normal hair shedding occurs at an average daily rate of:
    a) 75–150 hairs
    b) 90–120 hairs
    c) 20–40 hairs
    d) 90–110 hairs ____

44. The hair and scalp are kept in a soft and pliable condition by secretions of:
    a) hormones
    b) sebum
    c) keratin
    d) enzymes ____

45. The number of hairs per square inch is called hair:
    a) texture
    b) pigment
    c) melanin
    d) density ____

46. Wet normal hair can stretch its natural length about:
    a) 10%–15%
    b) 20%–25%
    c) 40%–50%
    d) 90%–100% ____

47. Dry normal hair can stretch to about:
    a) 20% its natural length
    b) 50% its natural length
    c) 75% its natural length
    d) none of the above ____

48. Canities is the technical term for:
    a) black hair
    b) brown hair
    c) cut hair
    d) gray hair ____

49. Trichoptilosis is the technical name for:
    a) beaded hair
    b) split hair ends
    c) superfluous hair
    d) brittle hair ____

50. Monilethrix is the technical name for:
    a) beaded hair
    b) brittle hair
    c) ringed hair
    d) knotted hair ____

51. Superfluous hair, or abnormal development of hair on the body, is called:
    a) alopecia
    b) hypertrichosis
    c) canities
    d) monilethrix ____

52. Fragilitas crinium is the technical name for:
    a) beaded hair
    b) superfluous hair
    c) knotted hair
    d) brittle hair ____

53. An abnormal development of hair on areas of the body that normally bear only downy hair is called all of the following EXCEPT:
a) hypertrichosis
b) superfluous
c) lanugo
d) hirsuties
____

54. Hirsuties is another name for:
a) fragilitas crinium
b) trichorrhexis nodosa
c) trichoptilosis
d) hypertrichosis
____

55. Another name for dandruff is:
a) alopecia
b) steatoma
c) pityriasis
d) dermatitis
____

56. Dandruff is generally believed to be:
a) an allergy
b) nonpathogenic
c) noncontagious
d) infectious
____

57. Long-neglected dandruff may lead to:
a) tinea
b) scabies
c) baldness
d) psoriasis
____

58. Small, white scales that usually appear on the scalp and hair are a sign of:
a) dermatitis
b) eczema
c) alopecia
d) pityriasis
____

59. The dry type of dandruff is known as pityriasis:
a) steatoides
b) capitis simplex
c) psoriasis
d) erysipelas
____

60. The greasy or waxy type of dandruff is known as pityriasis:
a) steatoides
b) psoriasis
c) erysipelas
d) capitis simplex
____

61. Alopecia is the technical term for any abnormal form of:
a) hair loss
b) skin inflammation
c) oil gland disorder
d) sweat gland disorder
____

62. Baldness in spots is known as alopecia:
a) adnata
b) senilis
c) areata
d) dynamica
____

63. Hair loss beginning before middle age is called alopecia:
a) senilis
b) adnata
c) prematura
d) universalis
____

64. Permanent hair loss in old age is called alopecia:
a) areata
b) senilis
c) adnata
d) dynamica
____

65. Alopecia areata occurs most frequently after an injury to the:
a) circulatory system
b) muscular system
c) nervous system
d) digestive system
____

66. The natural shedding of hair occurs most frequently in:
    a) the winter
    b) young people
    c) extreme cold
    d) the spring
    ___

67. The medical term for ringworm is:
    a) seborrhea
    b) tinea
    c) canities
    d) naevus
    ___

68. Ringworm is dangerous because it is:
    a) noncontagious
    b) noninfectious
    c) contagious
    d) benign
    ___

69. Pediculosis is a condition caused by:
    a) head lice
    b) itch mite
    c) a furuncle
    d) ringworm
    ___

70. Scabies is a contagious animal parasitic disease caused by:
    a) ringworm
    b) the itch mite
    c) dandruff
    d) a carbuncle
    ___

71. Tinea capitis is an infection involving the:
    a) sweat glands
    b) oil glands
    c) blood vessels
    d) hair follicles
    ___

72. The technical term for a boil is:
    a) scabies
    b) capitis
    c) tinea nodosa
    d) furuncle
    ___

73. Furuncle is an acute infection of the:
    a) oil glands
    b) sweat glands
    c) hair follicles
    d) sebaceous glands
    ___

74. The main purpose of a hair and scalp treatment is to:
    a) cure canities
    b) harden the texture of hair
    c) preserve the health of hair and scalp
    d) preserve the color of hair
    ___

75. Scalp massage is beneficial because it stimulates the:
    a) salivary gland
    b) blood circulation
    c) pituitary gland
    d) thyroid gland
    ___

76. A basic requisite for a healthy scalp is:
    a) an alkaline rinse
    b) a medicated rinse
    c) cleanliness
    d) a henna rinse
    ___

77. Frequent shampooing with strong soap may cause the scalp and hair to become:
    a) ulcerated
    b) oily
    c) dry
    d) thickened
    ___

78. After a scalp cream has been applied, expose the scalp to:
    a) ultraviolet light
    b) infrared lamp
    c) rays of blue light
    d) actinic rays
    ___

79. When damaged hair and a dry, tight scalp exist, recommend:
    a) a dry powder shampoo   c) restyling of the hair
    b) a dry liquid shampoo   d) scalp treatments   ____

80. An important part of a scalp treatment is proper:
    a) scalp tightening   c) hair brushing
    b) combing of hair   d) color rinsing   ____

81. A tight scalp can be made more flexible by:
    a) an egg dry shampoo   c) a tar shampoo
    b) scalp manipulations   d) an antiseptic shampoo   ____

82. Dust and dirt may be removed by:
    a) frequent bleachings   c) hair brushing
    b) haircolor   d) dry shampoos   ____

83. Scalp massage should be given to a normal scalp about:
    a) every three weeks   c) once a month
    b) once a week   d) every six months   ____

84. Scalp treatments are beneficial to clients because they promote:
    a) cavities   c) an increase in the hair's
                                  porosity
    b) a healthy scalp   d) pityriasis steatoides   ____

85. The common causes of dandruff are improper diet, neglect, and:
    a) poor circulation   c) oil shampoos
    b) frequent shampooing   d) cream rinses   ____

86. A very tight scalp may be made more flexible by proper brush-
    ing and the application of:
    a) a soapless shampoo   c) a gray rinse
    b) scalp manipulations   d) a sulfonated shampoo   ____

87. Hair brushing is beneficial because it:
    a) tightens scalp muscles c) stimulates blood circulation
    b) lightens the hair   d) preserves hair color   ____

88. One important benefit of scalp manipulations is that they:
    a) irrigate the scalp   c) remove sebum
    b) break hair ends   d) stimulate the flow of blood ____

89. Dry and damaged hair can be greatly improved by:
    a) emulsifying   c) shampooing
    b) conditioning   d) shaving   ____

90. It is not advisable to give a scalp treatment before a:
    a) hair relaxing treatment c) shampoo and set
    b) facial   d) hair shaping   ____

91. Brushing the hair before a scalp treatment helps to remove:
    a) dirt and dust   c) hair ends
    b) hair color   d) luster and sheen   ____

92. Scalp manipulations are valuable because they stimulate the:
    a) pituitary gland   c) blood circulation
    b) arrector pili   d) follicles   ____

93. The primary purpose of a scalp treatment is to preserve the:
    a) health of hair and scalp c) shaft and medulla
    b) hair's color and texture d) cortex and cuticle   ____

94. In order to soothe the client's tensions, massage movements
    must be given with a:
    a) hacking movement   c) vigorous manipulation
    b) continuous even motion   d) petrissage movement   ____

95. In addition to keeping the scalp and hair in a clean and healthy
    condition, regular scalp treatments help slow down:
    a) acne   c) baldness
    b) comedones   d) common colds   ____

96. The appearance of white scales on the head or scalp is an
    indication of:
    a) seborrhea   c) dandruff
    b) milia   d) comedones   ____

97. The more common causes of dandruff are improper diet, un-
    cleanliness, and:
    a) overactive sebaceous   c) underactive sebaceous
       glands   glands
    b) poor circulation   d) weak arrector pili
                                   muscles   ____

98. Moisturizing and emollient creams are used when treating a/an:
    a) dry scalp   c) acne condition
    b) oily scalp   d) seborrhea condition   ____

99. Hair lotions containing astringents may be applied only after the
    application of:
    a) high-frequency current   c) infrared current
    b) creams or ointments   d) setting lotions   ____

100. A corrective hair treatment deals with the:
    a) scalp   c) arrector pili
    b) hair shaft   d) medulla   ____

101. A condition of premature baldness or excessive loss of hair is
    referred to as:
    a) pityriasis   c) alopecia
    b) seborrhea   d) canities   ____

102. Alopecia areata is a disorder causing:
    a) premature baldness   c) old-age baldness
    b) baldness in spots   d) complete baldness   ____

Draping

1. The first consideration of the cosmetologist always should be the:
   a) fee to be charged
   b) protection of the client
   c) time consumed
   d) client's tip
   ____

2. The cosmetologist's primary responsibility is to protect the client from:
   a) overpaying
   b) loud noises
   c) injury
   d) competitors
   ____

3. An important part of the cosmetologist's service to the client is:
   a) reporting of news
   b) gabbing
   c) gossiping
   d) draping
   ____

4. In protecting the client's skin and clothing, proper draping is considered to be:
   a) an extra service
   b) a glamorous service
   c) completely unnecessary
   d) the first part of protection
   ____

5. Draping is designed to accomplish the objective of:
   a) protecting the client
   b) increasing the charges
   c) preventing client movement
   d) overcoming fatigue
   ____

6. The neck strip or towel is used to prevent:
   a) the client from perspiring
   b) the cape from touching the skin
   c) complete saturation of the hair
   d) an unpleasant feeling to the client
   ____

7. Every effort must be made to prevent the cape from touching the skin because it could be:
   a) cold to the skin
   b) a carrier of disease
   c) slightly damp
   d) disagreeable to touch
   ____

8. The neck strip or towel is used for client's protection and:
   a) esthetic reasons
   b) security reasons
   c) sanitary reasons
   d) monetary reasons
   ____

9. Before draping, clients should:
   a) wash their hands
   b) remove their jewelry
   c) brush through their hair
   d) remove their shoes and stockings
   ____

10. When draping for thermal curling or waving, it is wise to use a:
    a) cotton or linen cape
    b) plastic cape
    c) rubber cape
    d) very short cape
    ____

11. Draping for a comb-out should include:
    a) a towel at the neck
    b) use of a shampoo cape
    c) two towels around the neck
    d) a neck strip under the cape
    ____

Shampooing, Rinsing, and Conditioning

1. The main purpose of shampoos is to:
   a) style hair easier
   b) cleanse the hair and scalp
   c) treat alopecia areata
   d) soften the scalp
   _____

2. Before applying the shampoo, wet the hair with:
   a) cold water
   b) hot water
   c) warm water
   d) ice water
   _____

3. Strong alkaline shampoos make hair:
   a) soft and silky
   b) dry and brittle
   c) color fast
   d) easier to comb
   _____

4. Rainwater or water that has been chemically treated is _____ water.
   a) soft
   b) hard
   c) mineral
   d) carbonated
   _____

5. After a regular shampoo, rinse away all the soap from the hair with:
   a) a cold rinse
   b) cold water
   c) hot water
   d) a strong spray
   _____

6. Thorough brushing of the scalp and hair should NOT be given before a/an:
   a) chemical service
   b) shampoo
   c) haircut
   d) scalp treatment
   _____

7. What should be used when massaging and lathering the client's scalp and hair during a shampoo?
   a) the cushions of the fingers
   b) your fingernails
   c) the palm of the hand
   d) the thumbs only
   _____

8. During rinsing, one finger should be over the edge of the spray nozzle in order to:
   a) monitor the water temperature
   b) control the nozzle's direction
   c) determine the water pressure
   d) hold the nozzle in place
   _____

9. The term pH stands for:
   a) potential hydrogen
   b) parts of hydroxide
   c) a natural balance
   d) phosphorus and hydrogen
   _____

10. What type of shampoo is used on clients whose health does not permit them to receive a wet shampoo? A _____ shampoo.
    a) medicated
    b) conditioning
    c) powder dry
    d) highlighting
    _____

11. A powder dry shampoo should be recommended if a client:
   a) desires a color rinse
   b) cannot get their hair wet
   c) has hair that tangles
   d) has lightened hair
   _____

12. Brittle or dry hair should be cleansed with a/an:
   a) tint shampoo
   b) drab shampoo
   c) acid-balanced shampoo
   d) dry shampoo
   _____

13. Clients should be referred to a physician if they have:
   a) canities
   b) an infectious disease
   c) monlethrix
   d) a noninfectious disease
   _____

14. For hair and scalp cleanliness, the hair should be shampooed:
   a) every day
   b) every other day
   c) as often as necessary
   d) once a month
   _____

15. It is never advisable to brush the hair before giving a/an:
   a) cream shampoo
   b) permanent wave
   c) hair rinse
   d) acid-balanced shampoo
   _____

16. Acid rinses are given to:
   a) remove soap scum
   b) add color to hair
   c) remove yellow streaks from gray hair
   d) open the cuticle layer
   _____

17. What coats the hair to make it slick and smooth?
   a) cream rinse
   b) medicated shampoo
   c) acid rinse
   d) wig shampoo
   _____

18. A rinse that helps close and harden the cuticle imbrications after a tint or toner application is a/an:
   a) acid-balanced rinse
   b) alkaline rinse
   c) henna rinse
   d) medicated rinse
   _____

19. Color rinses give a:
   a) lighter shade to dark hair
   b) temporary color to hair
   c) curl to the hair
   d) permanent color to hair
   _____

20. A rinse that is formulated to make tangled hair easier to comb is a:
   a) medicated rinse
   b) reconditioning rinse
   c) nonstrip rinse
   d) cream rinse
   _____

21. A shampoo that has a pH of 5.5 is considered to be a/an:
   a) neutral product
   b) harsh shampoo
   c) alkaline
   d) acid
   _____

22. Minor dandruff conditions may be controlled by:
   a) plain water rinses
   b) medicated shampoos
   c) cream rinses
   d) color rinses
   _____

23. An acid rinse is important in helping to:
   a) remove soap scum
   b) prevent color fading
   c) change color
   d) curl hair
   _____

24. A medicated rinse is used to control:
    a) coarseness   c) short ends
    b) fineness   d) dandruff   ____

25. A rinse that is designed to temporarily color the hair is a/an:
    a) cream rinse   c) color rinse
    b) tartaric rinse   d) acid rinse   ____

Haircutting

1. The hair must be damp if hair thinning is done with:
   a) shears
   b) clippers
   c) a razor
   d) thinning scissors ____

2. Coarse hair should never be cut too close to the:
   a) sides
   b) hair shaft
   c) cuticle
   d) scalp ____

3. Modern hairstyles are designed to accentuate the client's:
   a) good points
   b) physical strength
   c) hair color
   d) poor features ____

4. The thinning of hair involves:
   a) cutting it straight off
   b) blunt cutting
   c) decreasing its bulk
   d) trimming the ends ____

5. The shortening of hair in a graduated effect is known as:
   a) clipping
   b) singeing
   c) tapering
   d) back-combing ____

6. The process used in thinning the hair with scissors is known as:
   a) clipping
   b) razor cutting
   c) layer cutting
   d) slithering ____

7. Cutting the hair in graduated lengths from the nape of the neck toward the crown of the head is known as:
   a) layer cutting
   b) razor cutting
   c) club cutting
   d) shingling ____

8. When holding the scissor during a haircut, which finger should be placed into the ring of the still blade?
   a) index
   b) middle or center
   c) ring or third
   d) thumb ____

9. In selecting the proper hairstyle, the cosmetologist should take into consideration the client's:
   a) hairpieces
   b) French lacing
   c) facial contour
   d) hair oiliness ____

10. The first step in successful hair shaping is to:
    a) color the hair
    b) section the hair
    c) effilate the hair
    d) feather the hair ____

11. The tip of the index finger is braced near the pivot of the scissors to give the stylist:
    a) more speed
    b) better control
    c) greater vision
    d) guidelines ____

12. An important factor in deciding how close to the head the hair may be thinned is the hair's:
    a) elasticity
    b) color
    c) texture
    d) stream ____

13. The type of hair that can be thinned closest to the scalp is:
    a) fine
    b) medium
    c) coarse
    d) damaged ____

14. Hair that should be thinned furthest from the scalp is:
    a) fine
    b) medium
    c) coarse
    d) tinted ____

15. Effilating is another term for:
    a) slithering
    b) clipping
    c) shingling
    d) club cutting ____

16. The foundation for a successful hairstyle is a good:
    a) coloring
    b) streaking
    c) lightening
    d) cut ____

17. If the hair is thinned near the ends of the strands, it will be:
    a) shapeless
    b) blunt
    c) blunt cut
    d) shingled ____

18. The method of cutting hair straight across without tapering is referred to as:
    a) slithering
    b) feather edging
    c) razor cutting
    d) blunt cutting ____

19. Hair may be thinned with scissors, thinning shears, or:
    a) the clippers
    b) a razor
    c) the shank
    d) the pivot ____

20. Before cutting overly curly hair, it should be shampooed, dried, and:
    a) cut with a thinning shears
    b) setting lotion should be applied to the hair
    c) cut with a razor
    d) an emollient product should be applied to the scalp and hair ____

21. Haircutting requires considerable skill, knowledge, and:
    a) endurance
    b) practice
    c) money
    d) chatter ____

Finger Waving

1. The best results in finger waving are obtained with hair that is:
   a) straight
   b) naturally wavy
   c) frizzy
   d) kinky _____

2. When finger waving, use:
   a) hair lacquer
   b) ammonia water
   c) cold wave lotion
   d) wave setting lotion _____

3. When giving a finger wave, what makes the hair more pliable and holds it in place?
   a) a cream rinse
   b) wave setting lotion
   c) hair lacquer
   d) a neutralizer _____

4. The choice of wave setting lotion should be determined by:
   a) its drying qualities
   b) its color
   c) the texture of client's hair
   d) its lacquer consistency _____

5. A good finger waving lotion:
   a) dries very slowly
   b) colors the hair
   c) is harmless to the hair
   d) lightens the hair _____

6. Before finger waving, find the:
   a) new hair growth
   b) receding hairline
   c) natural wave
   d) line of demarcation _____

7. A finger wave should harmonize with the client's:
   a) skin complexion
   b) clothing style
   c) fingernails
   d) head shape and facial features _____

8. When giving a finger wave, avoid:
   a) the use of excessive lotion
   b) directing hair toward its natural growth
   c) pushing the ridges firmly in place
   d) having the comb penetrate to the scalp _____

9. With a side part hairstyle, finger waving should start on the:
   a) thin side of the hair
   b) back of the head
   c) heavy side of the hair
   d) crown part of the head _____

10. A finger wave lasts longer when the hair is molded:
    a) in very high ridges
    b) in the direction of the natural growth
    c) in very low ridges
    d) opposite to the inclination of natural growth _____

11. After a finger wave, what should be the condition of the hair before it is combed out?
    a) thoroughly dried
    b) thoroughly lubricated
    c) quite damp
    d) oily _____

12. To emphasize the ridge of a finger wave
    a) press the teeth of
       the comb against the head
    b) use the comb and
       back of hand
    c) press the index and
       middle fingers against
       the head
    d) push the hair down
       with the fingers   ____

13. After a finger wave, excessive drying of the hair will:
    a) cause a dry condition
       of the hair and scalp
    b) add oil to hair and scalp
    c) make the wave longer
       lasting
    d) upset the wave   ____

14. The term "shadow wave" indicates a hairsetting with:
    a) high ridges
    b) sharp ridges
    c) low ridges
    d) deep waves   ____

15. The ridge and wave of each section in finger waving should match:
    a) the crown
    b) the new growth
    c) evenly
    d) the hair ends   ____

16. To protect the client's forehead and ears from intense dryer heat, use cotton, gauze, or:
    a) clippies
    b) paper protectors
    c) hairnets
    d) waving lotion   ____

Wet Hairstyling

1. It is important that a cosmetologist know basic hairstyling in order to:
   a) develop elasticity in the hair
   b) analyze client's hair as to fineness or coarseness
   c) create fashionable hairstyles
   d) make the hair more manageable
   _____

2. Before giving a shampoo, it is advisable to:
   a) recondition the hair
   b) style the hair
   c) color the hair
   d) examine the hair
   _____

3. The process of removing tangles from the hair should start in the:
   a) crown area
   b) hairline area
   c) nape area
   d) forehead area
   _____

4. A curl that decreases in size toward the hair ends is called a/an _____ curl.
   a) open center
   b) forward
   c) spiral
   d) closed center
   _____

5. To obtain successful results in hairstyling, the hair must be:
   a) coarse in texture
   b) in good condition
   c) completely dry
   d) set on medium rollers
   _____

6. For long-lasting and spring curls, the hair strand is ribboned and stretched, and each curl is:
   a) directed away from the face
   b) wound smoothly
   c) directed toward the face
   d) placed in a haphazard manner
   _____

7. The type of hair that is best suited for pin curling is:
   a) straight coarse hair
   b) natural or permanent-waved hair
   c) fine curly hair
   d) wiry, overcurly hair
   _____

8. The three principal parts of a pin curl are its base, circle, and:
   a) texture
   b) elasticity
   c) stem
   d) mobility
   _____

9. The immovable part of the curl attached to the scalp is the:
   a) stem
   b) base
   c) circle
   d) arc
   _____

10. That part of a pin curl found between the base and the first arc of the circle is known as the:
    a) circle
    b) stem
    c) pivot
    d) strand
    _____

11. The curl obtains its direction, action, and mobility from its:
    a) pivot   c) circle
    b) base   d) stem   ____

12. The width and strength of the wave are governed by the pin curl's:
    a) size   c) stem
    b) pivot   d) mobility   ____

13. The mobility of a pin curl is determined by its:
    a) base   c) pivot
    b) stem   d) circle   ____

14. Curl mobility is classified as half-stem, full-stem, and:
    a) round-stem   c) no-stem
    b) narrow-stem   d) wide-stem   ____

15. A firm, immovable position, permitting only the circle of the curl to move, is created by a:
    a) no-stem curl   c) full-stem curl
    b) half-stem curl   d) round-stem curl   ____

16. The half-stem formation permits the circle to:
    a) move toward its base   c) remain immobile on
                                  its base
    b) move away from its base d) curl up on its base   ____

17. When the hairstyle requires a great deal of mobility, use the:
    a) full-stem curl   c) no-stem curl
    b) half-stem curl   d) round-stem curl   ____

18. To avoid splits or breaks at the front or facial hairline, use:
    a) triangular bases   c) circular bases
    b) square bases   d) round bases   ____

19. If a fluffy comb-out is desired on fine hair, use pin curls with:
    a) open centers   c) no-stems
    b) half-stems   d) closed centers   ____

20. Pin curls that are placed behind the ridgeline of a shaping are called:
    a) roller curls   c) pivot curls
    b) ridge curls   d) sculpture curls   ____

21. Curls formed in the opposite direction to the movement of the hands of a clock are considered to be:
    a) clockwise   c) sculptured
    b) counterclockwise   d) cascades   ____

22. The size of a pin curl will determine a wave's:
    a) size   c) direction
    b) depth   d) ridges   ____

23. A wave formed by alternating finger waves and pin curls is called a:
   a) loose wave
   b) stand-up wave
   c) skip wave
   d) full wave ____

24. To obtain wide, smooth-flowing vertical waves on the sides of the head, recommend a:
   a) narrow wave
   b) stand-up wave
   c) tight wave
   d) skip wave ____

25. The cascade curl is also known as the:
   a) bob curl
   b) molded curl
   c) stand-up curl
   d) pivot curl ____

26. Parting the hair should be determined by the client's facial type and the desired:
   a) curl base
   b) curl pivot
   c) hairstyle
   d) hair color ____

27. Most failures in combing out hairstyles are due primarily to:
   a) skip waving
   b) hair slithering
   c) improperly set hair
   d) the use of a hair brush ____

28. A stand-up curl is sometimes referred to as a/an:
   a) cascade curl
   b) ridge curl
   c) elongated stem curl
   d) open end curl ____

29. In anchoring pin curls, all of the following are true EXCEPT:
   a) clips are inserted from the open end of the shaping
   b) clips are inserted from the closed end of the shaping
   c) it is important not to disturb the shaping
   d) cotton should be placed between the skin and the clip while drying ____

30. A strand of hair designed to be a base for a wave is a:
   a) curl
   b) shaping
   c) ridge
   d) section ____

31. Carefully removing a section of hair from a pin curl shaping is referred to as:
   a) sectioning
   b) slicing
   c) molding
   d) directing ____

32. The type of face that is most becoming with any type of hairstyle worn is the:
   a) oblong type
   b) pear-shaped type
   c) oval type
   d) diamond type ____

33. Covering the neck with soft waves or curls is recommended for a client with:
   a) wide cheekbones
   b) a long, thin neck
   c) a narrow chin
   d) a short, thick neck ____

34. Hair spray is applied after a comb-out in order to:
    a) hold the hairstyle in place
    b) make the hair easier to set
    c) prevent snarling of the hair
    d) make the hair more pliable
    ____

35. To control the hair ends when winding the hair on rollers, you may use:
    a) hair spray
    b) end papers
    c) roller pins
    d) hair clips
    ____

36. To form a cushion or base during a comb-out, the hairstylist may use:
    a) thinning
    b) stripping
    c) back-combing
    d) feathering
    ____

37. A curl that is wound like a roller curl without using a roller is a:
    a) carved curl
    b) ridge curl
    c) barrel curl
    d) French curl
    ____

38. The setting pattern of large, smooth pin curls into two long vertical shapings at the back of the head will result in a:
    a) French twist
    b) page boy
    c) beehive
    d) halo
    ____

39. Combing the short hairs of a strand towards the scalp is known as:
    a) effileing
    b) feathering
    c) slithering
    d) back-combing
    ____

40. A section of hair that has been molded into a design to serve as a base for a curl or wave pattern is a:
    a) base
    b) stem
    c) shaping
    d) bouffant
    ____

41. Brushing the short hairs of a strand toward the scalp is called:
    a) French lacing
    b) back-combing
    c) ruffing
    d) teasing
    ____

42. A shaping directed toward the face is a:
    a) backward shaping
    b) horizontal shaping
    c) reverse shaping
    d) forward shaping
    ____

43. A roller that has one end smaller than the other is known as a _____ roller.
    a) tapered
    b) cylinder
    c) mesh
    d) concave
    ____

44. Pin curls sliced out of a shaping without disturbing the shaping are called:
    a) French curls
    b) carved curls
    c) tension curls
    d) anchor curls
    ____

45. The concave profile is indicated by a:
    a) receding chin
    b) low forehead
    c) prominent nose
    d) prominent chin

    ___

46. A receding forehead and chin are typical of the:
    a) straight profile
    b) convex profile
    c) concave profile
    d) oval profile

    ___

47. The perfect shaped head is considered to be:
    a) elliptical
    b) oblong
    c) round
    d) oval

    ___

Thermal Hairstyling

1. For white, lightened, or tinted hair, it is advisable to use thermal irons that are:
   a) very hot
   b) lukewarm
   c) cold
   d) steaming hot

2. Electric vaporizing irons should not be used on pressed hair because they cause the hair to:
   a) revert
   b) break
   c) straighten
   d) discolor

3. Overheated irons often are ruined because the metal loses its:
   a) color
   b) balance
   c) temper
   d) shape

4. The use of hot thermal irons on chemically straightened hair will cause hair:
   a) to revert to curly state
   b) growth
   c) discoloration
   d) damage

5. The required temperature of heated thermal irons depends on:
   a) the type of irons selected
   b) texture of the hair
   c) cosmetologist's speed
   d) the size of the heater

6. Fishhook hair ends are caused when the:
   a) irons are too hot
   b) hair ends protrude over the irons
   c) curl is started too high
   d) curl is started too low

7. To hold an even temperature, thermal irons should be made of the best quality:
   a) plastic
   b) zinc
   c) steel
   d) magnesium

8. The temperature of heated thermal irons is tested on:
   a) a strand of hair
   b) a piece of tissue paper
   c) a damp cloth
   d) wax paper

9. The art of creating curls with the aid of heated irons and a comb is known as:
   a) pony tail curling
   b) spiral curling
   c) thermal curling
   d) swivel curling

10. The thermal iron curl that provides maximum lift or volume is the:
    a) off base curl
    b) volume-base curl
    c) quarter base curl
    d) half base curl

11. The person credited for being the originator of thermal waving was:
    a) English
    b) Hungarian
    c) Belgian
    d) French

12. A thermal comb should be made of:
    a) plastic
    c) steel
    b) hard rubber
    d) soft rubber ———

13. To give a finished appearance to hair ends, use:
    a) off base curls
    c) volume base curls
    b) end curls
    d) full base curls ———

14. To ensure a good thermal curl or wave, the hair must be:
    a) bleached
    c) clean
    b) bulky
    d) reverted ———

15. The waving area of thermal irons consists of two parts, the solid round rod and:
    a) revolving handles
    c) the shank
    b) corquignole part
    d) the shell ———

16. Volume thermal irons curls are created to provide the finished hairstyle with:
    a) tension
    c) lift
    b) indentation
    d) depth ———

17. In blow-dry styling, better waves and curls are produced with hair that has a:
    a) skip
    c) roller curl
    b) natural wave
    d) thermal wave ———

18. Blow-dry curling should be performed with caution on hair that has been:
    a) permanently waved
    c) colored
    b) brushed
    d) finger waved ———

19. The technique of drying and styling damp hair in one operation is called:
    a) croquignole styling
    c) thermal styling
    b) thermal irons styling
    d) blow-dry styling ———

20. An electrical device especially designed for drying and styling the hair in a single operation is a:
    a) thermal dryer
    c) blow-dryer
    b) hood dryer
    d) curl dryer ———

21. In blow-dry styling, the blower is directed:
    a) toward the scalp
    c) toward the face
    b) away from the scalp
    d) on the scalp ———

22. In order to assure complete dryness of hair, the blower is used in a/an:
    a) back-and-forth movement
    c) straight line movement
    b) in-and-out movement
    d) stop-and-go movement ———

23. When in operation, the blow-dryer produces a steady stream of temperature-controlled:
    a) vapors
    c) water
    b) air
    d) steam ———

24. Excessive hairstyling by the blow-drying method may cause dryness and:
    a) deep waves   c) discoloration
    b) split ends   d) shadow waves   _____

25. Excessive blow-drying may result in the loss of:
    a) elasticity   c) color
    b) texture   d) density   _____

26. In blow-dry styling, before the hair is combed out, it must be thoroughly:
    a) brushed   c) cooled
    b) tangled   d) permed   _____

27. Setting and drying the hair with the use of electric comb and styling comb is called:
    a) marcel waving   c) French waving
    b) thermal waving   d) air waving   _____

28. In air waving, the hair is styled after it has been shaped, shampooed, and:
    a) colored   c) thermal waved
    b) permanent waved   d) towel dried   _____

29. The styling of hair with an air waver is performed in the same manner as:
    a) thermal waving   c) chemical waving
    b) blow-out waving   d) finger waving   _____

30. For successful blow-dry styling, the air should be directed from the scalp area toward the:
    a) hair ends   c) nape
    b) crown area   d) forehead   _____

Permanent Waving

1. Vigorously brushing the hair before a permanent wave may cause:
   a) hair discoloration
   b) scalp tightening
   c) healthy hair to fall out
   d) scalp irritations   ——

2. Before a permanent wave, a mild shampoo should be accompanied by:
   a) gentle scalp manipulations
   b) kneading scalp manipulations
   c) vibratory scalp manipulations
   d) stimulating scalp manipulations   ——

3. Before starting a permanent wave, the hair is shampooed and:
   a) lubricated
   b) brushed
   c) towel dried
   d) lightened   ——

4. For a successful permanent wave, it is necessary to have the hair properly:
   a) tinted
   b) cut
   c) colored
   d) lightened   ——

5. In giving a permanent wave, always follow:
   a) with a dry shampoo
   b) with a tar shampoo
   c) with a quick lightener
   d) the manufacturer's instructions   ——

6. A method of wrapping a permanent wave that is suitable for extra long hair is the:
   a) double halo method
   b) piggyback method
   c) dropped crown method
   d) single halo method   ——

7. The proper way to wind the hair for a permanent wave is to:
   a) bunch the hair in the center of the rod and stretch it in winding
   b) twist the hair and wind it without tension
   c) distribute hair evenly on rod and stretch it in winding
   d) distribute hair evenly on rod and wind it smoothly and without stretching   ——

8. In permanent waving, a longer processing time is usually required for hair that is:
   a) lightened
   b) tinted
   c) porous
   d) resistant   ——

9. Special perming prewrapping lotions are designed to:
   a) equalize the hair's porosity
   b) add color to the hair
   c) be used on clients with canities
   d) close the cuticle layer   ——

10. The main active ingredient in acid-balanced waving lotions is:
    a) ammonium thioglycolate
    b) glyceryl monothioglycolate
    c) sodium hydroxide
    d) hydrogen peroxide   ——

11. If the fastening band is twisted or stretched too tightly on permanent-waving curling rods, it may cause a:
    a) frizzy curl
    b) springy curl
    c) hair breakage
    d) resilient curl ____

12. In order to determine in advance how the client's hair will react to the permanent-waving process, give:
    a) a conditioning treatment
    b) saturating tests
    c) blocking arrangements
    d) a test curl ____

13. End papers used in wrapping hair ends for a permanent wave must be:
    a) nonporous
    b) waterproof
    c) porous
    d) neutralized ____

14. The waving lotion used on the hair has a:
    a) hardening action
    b) softening action
    c) lubricating action
    d) stiffening action ____

15. The waving lotion is used for as long as it is required by both the condition of the hair and its:
    a) color
    b) melanin content
    c) pigment
    d) texture and porosity ____

16. During the processing time in permanent waving, the hair tends to:
    a) contract
    b) soften
    c) darken
    d) harden ____

17. Excessive tapering before a permanent wave may result in hair ends that are:
    a) frizzy
    b) straight
    c) curled in
    d) curled out ____

18. A longer processing time in permanent waving is usually required for:
    a) tinted hair
    b) porous hair
    c) resistant hair
    d) lightened hair ____

19. A shorter processing time in permanent waving is usually required for hair that is:
    a) lightened
    b) resistant
    c) wiry
    d) coarse ____

20. The size of the curl or wave in permanent waving is controlled by the:
    a) size of the perm rod
    b) cold wave solution
    c) neutralizer
    d) end papers used ____

21. Overprocessing in permanent waving usually produces:
    a) loose curls
    b) elastic curls
    c) frizzy curls
    d) tight curls ____

22. Hair that readily absorbs a permanent waving solution is best described as being:
   a) porous
   b) glassy
   c) resistant
   d) wiry
   ____

23. The ability of hair to absorb liquids is its:
   a) porosity
   b) texture
   c) elasticity
   d) density
   ____

24. The diameter of the individual hair and its degree of coarseness or fineness are its:
   a) density
   b) texture
   c) porosity
   d) resiliency
   ____

25. The processing time for any permanent wave depends on the hair texture and its:
   a) alkalinity
   b) porosity
   c) elasticity
   d) resiliency
   ____

26. One reason for success in permanent waving is due to:
   a) tight winding of hair
   b) underprocessing of hair
   c) complete saturation of the hair
   d) overprocessing of hair
   ____

27. Permanent waving combines manual skill and a/an:
   a) cataphoresis process
   b) galvanism process
   c) chemical process
   d) anilinic process
   ____

28. Stopping the action of the permanent-wave solution and fixing the curl are accomplished with:
   a) a hair tint
   b) an oil lightener
   c) 70% alcohol
   d) a neutralizer
   ____

29. The permanent-wave neutralizer is designed to stop the action of the waving lotion and:
   a) relax curled hair
   b) loosen curled hair
   c) soften curled hair
   d) harden curled hair
   ____

30. Thorough rinsing is essential as part of the prepermanent shampoo procedure because it helps to:
   a) equalize porosity
   b) make hair colorfast
   c) block the hair
   d) slow down processing
   ____

31. In permanent waving, hair that is too curly when wet and frizzy when dry indicates that:
   a) it was underprocessed
   b) it was overprocessed
   c) too much water was used
   d) too much oil was used
   ____

32. Hair may darken or break if a permanent-wave lotion is applied to hair previously treated with:
   a) henna
   b) an aniline tint
   c) a metallic tint
   d) a lightener
   ____

33. Winding the hair smoothly and without stretching around the permanent-wave rods allows the hair to:
   a) change color during processing
   b) darken during processing
   c) expand during processing
   d) thin out during processing   ____

34. If a permanent-wave lotion accidentally drips on the skin, the cosmetologist should immediately apply:
   a) aniline
   b) formalin
   c) neutralizer
   d) more lotion   ____

35. The use of porous end papers helps to eliminate the possibility of:
   a) overprocessing
   b) saturation
   c) fishhooks
   d) underprocessing   ____

36. The waving solution contains:
   a) a quaternary ammonium compound
   b) denatured ammonium
   c) ammonium thioglycolate
   d) borax ammonium   ____

37. A very mild strength waving solution should be recommended for:
   a) fine hair
   b) tinted hair
   c) coarse hair
   d) virgin hair   ____

38. The most important step before giving a permanent wave is:
   a) proper hair lightening
   b) a complete color rinse
   c) proper processing
   d) analysis of client's hair   ____

39. Correct wrapping in permanent waving permits better:
   a) porosity
   b) blocking
   c) analysis
   d) saturation   ____

40. What is it called when heat is created chemically within the perm product?
   a) exothermic
   b) reducing agent
   c) endothermic
   d) underprocessing   ____

41. A weak or limp wave formation is the result of:
   a) overprocessing
   b) underprocessing
   c) resaturation
   d) test processing   ____

42. The pH of wave solutions made with ammonium thioglycolate is usually:
   a) acid
   b) alkaline
   c) chlorine
   d) oxidine   ____

43. Protect the client's face and neck during processing with a/an:
   a) hairnet
   b) cotton strips
   c) neck strip
   d) end paper   ____

44. Acid-balanced permanent-wave solutions have a pH range of:
   a) 8.3 to 9.4   c) 4.5 to 6.5
   b) 7.9 to 8.4   d) 7.0 to 7.9   ___

45. In acid-balanced permanent waving, damage to hair or skin is minimized because:
   a) waving lotion is used   c) harsh alkalis are not used
   b) concentrated heat is applied   d) permanent wave rods are used   ___

46. Acid-balanced permanent-wave solutions are activated by the application of:
   a) a neutralizer   c) ammonia
   b) heat   d) an alkali   ___

47. What is it called when a perm is activated by an outside heat force (such as a conventional hooded hair dryer)?
   a) acid-balanced   c) exothermic
   b) reducing agent   d) endothermic   ___

48. The procedure for acid-balanced permanent waving permits greater control and less possibility of:
   a) successful perming   c) curl control
   b) color fastness   d) over-processing   ___

49. Which bonds in the hair must be broken down to allow the perming process to occur?
   a) disulfide   c) salt
   b) hydrogen   d) cortex   ___

50. In acid-balanced permanent waving, processing begins as soon as the:
   a) lotion is applied   c) hair is saturated
   b) neutralizer is applied   d) heat is applied   ___

51. In acid-balanced permanent waving, heat is applied to:
   a) control hair color   c) prevent overprocessing
   b) speed up processing   d) slow down processing   ___

52. Acid-balanced and neutral permanent-wave lotions produce:
   a) deep and very tight waves   c) soft, natural-looking waves
   b) color streaks in the hair   d) shorter-lasting waves   ___

Haircoloring

1. The art and science of changing the color of hair is called:
   a) shampooing
   b) conditioning
   c) haircoloring
   d) temporary
   ____

2. A haircoloring process is:
   a) deep conditioning
   b) slithering
   c) neutralizing
   d) adding artifical pigment to natural hair
   ____

3. The terms "tinting" and "coloring" mean:
   a) the same thing
   b) brassiness
   c) opposites
   d) black roots
   ____

4. Decolorizing is another name for:
   a) color wheel
   b) hair lightening
   c) accents
   d) conditioning
   ____

5. Haircoloring is a profitable salon service as it means:
   a) short cuts
   b) quick services
   c) rich customers
   d) repeat business
   ____

6. Time, energy, study, and practice lead to:
   a) headaches
   b) success as a colorist
   c) more vacations
   d) skin rashes
   ____

7. Concealing gray, promoting a more professional appearance, or making a fashion statement are all reasons clients request:
   a) new stylists
   b) conditioners
   c) haircolor services
   d) blunt cuts
   ____

8. A typical haircolor client today is likely to be a:
   a) man
   b) young woman
   c) teenager
   d) all of the above
   ____

9. The fastest growing category of haircoloring client is:
   a) men
   b) teenagers
   c) older women
   d) mothers
   ____

10. A professional-only haircoloring product surpasses home hair-colors in:
    a) price
    b) colors available
    c) performance and stability
    d) mistakes
    ____

11. The key to success in haircoloring is
    a) communication
    b) shampoo
    c) permanent tints
    d) rinsing
    ____

12. The stylist's primary information gathering tool is her/his:
    a) eyes
    b) manager
    c) textbooks
    d) assistant
    ____

13. Client's color tone and eye color are two items noted during a:
    a) shampoo
    b) perm service
    c) haircut
    d) haircolor consultation ____

14. A cosmetologist discovers a client's needs through:
    a) gossip
    b) listening
    c) mistakes
    d) many visits ____

15. The appearance of hair color is affected by:
    a) light
    b) skin tone
    c) glasses
    d) conditioners ____

16. Paper color charts, hair color swatchers, and magazines are items used during:
    a) art classes
    b) fashion show
    c) color consultation
    d) thermal hairstyling ____

17. A preliminary test given on a small section of hair to determine the mixture and development time is a:
    a) predisposition test
    b) patch test
    c) skin test
    d) strand test ____

18. The usual strand testing method is to apply color to:
    a) elbow fold
    b) back of knee
    c) ½" section in crown
    d) entire head ____

19. Before coloring hair with an aniline derivative product, you must perform a:
    a) permanent wave
    b) predisposition test
    c) leg waxing
    d) haircut ____

20. Patch test and skin test are other names for:
    a) predisposition test
    b) strand test
    c) spot conditioning
    d) spot perming ____

21. The area usually chosen for a skin test is either behind the ear or at the inner fold of the:
    a) knee
    b) arm
    c) wrist
    d) neck ____

22. A skin or patch test is left undisturbed for a period of:
    a) 24 hours
    b) 12 hours
    c) 6 hours
    d) 8 hours ____

23. Redness, swelling, burning, itching, or blisters are symptoms of:
    a) bug bites
    b) tight clothing
    c) allergic reaction
    d) poor hygiene ____

24. A skin test that results in an allergic reaction is said to be:
    a) negative
    b) positive
    c) inclusive
    d) hazardous ____

25. A negative skin test means that the aniline derivative tint may:
    a) not be safely used
    b) be safely used in six months
    c) be safely used immediately
    d) be safely used in one year ____

26. The consultation and record of services are written on a:
    a) yellow pad
    b) client record card
    c) pink paper
    d) blue card
    ____

27. A form required for some malpractice insurance is the:
    a) credit card slip
    b) record card
    c) release statement
    d) tax return
    ____

28. When analyzing hair condition, it is necessary to evaluate the hair's texture, porosity, and:
    a) style
    b) color
    c) density
    d) elasticity
    ____

29. The terms coarse, medium, and fine differentiate between large, medium, and small:
    a) diameters
    b) heads
    c) lengths
    d) rods
    ____

30. This hair texture has pigment grouped more tightly together:
    a) coarse
    b) medium
    c) fine
    d) large
    ____

31. A milder lightener can be used on fine hair because it is less:
    a) black
    b) resistant
    c) orange
    d) blue
    ____

32. Average responses to color products occur with:
    a) medium-textured hair
    b) fine hair
    c) coarse hair
    d) black hair
    ____

33. Color deposit is usually lighter on hair with this texture:
    a) medium
    b) well
    c) fine
    d) coarse
    ____

34. The numbers of hair per square inch on the scalp is called hair:
    a) texture
    b) color
    c) density
    d) loop
    ____

35. Long hair has been exposed for a longer period of time to:
    a) the elements
    b) clothing
    c) cutting
    d) vegetables
    ____

36. The shaft of older hair will have variations in:
    a) form
    b) porosity
    c) texture
    d) density
    ____

37. The smoother the hair form, the more:
    a) shampoo needed
    b) color product used
    c) light reflection
    d) tangles
    ____

38. A stronger tone may be needed on:
    a) bleached hair
    b) dry hair
    c) fine hair
    d) curly hair
    ____

39. The degree of lightness or darkness of a particular color is called the:
   a) texture
   b) level
   c) porosity
   d) form ____

40. The strength of the tonality in a color is called:
   a) intensity
   b) level
   c) porosity
   d) elasticity ____

41. Natural cool tones show no:
   a) blue and red
   b) black and white
   c) red or yellow
   d) white or yellow ____

42. Natural warm tones contain:
   a) red and yellow
   b) gray
   c) blue and violet
   d) orange and blue ____

43. Gray hair tends to be coarser and:
   a) finer
   b) less elastic
   c) softer
   d) dirtier ____

44. Gray hair is _____ to chemical services than pigmented hair.
   a) more resistant
   b) less resistant
   c) softer
   d) better suited ____

45. In gray hair, the nonpigmented melanin is located in the:
   a) eumelanin
   b) ends
   c) hair shaft
   d) roots ____

46. Sulfur-based medicines taken by a client can add warmth to:
   a) light blonde colors
   b) black hair
   c) red colors
   d) brunettes ____

47. Natural hair color can be darkened by:
   a) carrots
   b) lemon juice
   c) high doses of vitamins
   d) conditioning ____

48. Two colors situated directly across from each other on the color wheel are known as _____ colors.
   a) quaternary
   b) primary
   c) tertiary
   d) complementary ____

49. What color base is used to neutralize a green cast in your client's hair?
   a) yellot
   b) blue
   c) red
   d) purple ____

50. Temporary rinses last:
   a) 5–6 shampoos
   b) 4 weeks
   c) until shampooed out
   d) until stripped out ____

51. A patch test is usually not necessary for:
   a) permanent hair tints
   b) aniline hair tints
   c) temporary colors
   d) compound dyes ____

52. Tints that are formulated to last four to six shampoos are applied without:
    a) peroxide
    b) blending
    c) coloring agents
    d) highlighting ____

53. Prelightening of the hair is necessary when using a:
    a) single application
    b) toner
    c) presoftener
    d) translucent stain ____

54. Haircolor rinses are colorings that are:
    a) permanent
    b) temporary
    c) semipermanent
    d) penetrating ____

55. A classification of color that uses a low-volume developer is:
    a) temporary
    b) deposit-only
    c) permanent
    d) polymer ____

56. Deposit-only colors last:
    a) 2–4 months
    b) 4–6 days
    c) 6–10 weeks
    d) 4–6 weeks ____

57. Henna is an example of a:
    a) vegetable tint
    b) mineral tint
    c) compound dye
    d) metallic dye ____

58. Henna colors the hair by:
    a) coating the medulla
    b) coating the hair shaft
    c) penetrating the cortex
    d) osmosis ____

59. To test for metallic salts, immerse a strand of hair in a solution of 20 volume peroxide and 28%:
    a) potassium persulfate
    b) thioglycolate
    c) ammonia water
    d) distilled water ____

60. A compound dye is a combination of vegetable tint with a:
    a) restorer tint
    b) metallic salt
    c) color rinse
    d) shampoo tint ____

61. Tints that lighten and deposit color in the hair shaft at one time require:
    a) a single application
    b) stablizing
    c) presoftening
    d) toning ____

62. Toners are used for:
    a) double-application tints
    b) single-application tints
    c) one-process tints
    d) certified colors ____

63. In permanent hair tinting, hydrogen peroxide is used as a:
    a) conditioner
    b) developer
    c) filler
    d) color rinse ____

64. Volume refers to the capacity of the:
    a) color pigment
    b) lightening agent
    c) filler
    d) hydrogen peroxide ____

65. Prelightening is required before applying a:
    a) temporary color   c) toner
    b) one-step color   d) tint   _____

66. Lighteners are classified as powder, oil, or:
    a) peroxide lighteners   c) suspension lighteners
    b) double power lighteners d) cream lighteners   _____

67. Hair lightening involves:
    a) adding artifical pigment to   c) removing pigment from the
       the natural hair color   hair
    b) restoring gray hair to its   d) adding artificial pigment to
       original color   prelightened hair   _____

68. To change the hair color to a much lighter shade, the hair should
    first be:
    a) presoftened   c) toned
    b) prelightened   d) neutralized   _____

69. Prelightening before applying a hair tint serves to:
    a) remove metallic dye   c) darken hair
    b) soften lightened hair d) increase hair porosity _____

70. White or gray hair requires some prelightening before applica-
    tion of a toner in order to:
    a) take out color   c) prevent hair breakage
    b) make it porous enough d) prevent scalp irritation
       to receive color   _____

71. A virgin head of hair is one that has:
    a) had a permanent wave   c) been tinted
    b) not been lightened or tinted d) been lightened _____

72. A hair lightener should never be given to a client if the:
    a) hair is permanently waved c) scalp has abrasions
    b) hair has been cut   d) hair is sun bleached _____

73. At what point from the scalp should the hair lightener first be
    applied for a virgin lightening treatment?
    a) ⅛–¼"   c) 1 ½–2"
    b) ½"   d) at the scalp   _____

74. The action of the prelightener continues as long as it is:
    a) thickened   c) kept moist
    b) kept dry   d) neutralized   _____

75. When the desired shade is reached, the lightener should be
    removed with:
    a) sulfonated oil   c) hydrogen peroxide
    b) cool water   d) hot water   _____

76. When you are ready to apply the hair tint, the client's hair and
    scalp should be:
    a) vigorously massaged   c) moistened with an alkali
    b) re-examined for abrasions d) given an ultraviolet rinse _____

77. Overlapping in the lightening process results in hair:
    a) breakage
    b) porosity
    c) retouching
    d) retention
    _____

78. Applying tint to small areas not colored evenly, in order to even results throughout, is known as:
    a) spot lightening
    b) developing
    c) frosting
    d) conditioning
    _____

79. What are toners?
    a) temporary tints
    b) pale, delicate permanent tints
    c) semipermanent tints
    d) metallic dyes
    _____

80. In a double-process application, a patch test is required for the:
    a) cream lightener
    b) toner
    c) hydrogen peroxide
    d) "quick" lightener
    _____

81. In a toner retouch, new growth must be _____ to same stage as for first toner application.
    a) conditioned
    b) prelightened
    c) colored
    d) curled
    _____

82. Any technique of partial lightening or coloring is called:
    a) bleaching
    b) painting
    c) stripping
    d) special effects highlighting
    _____

83. Special effects are created by strategically placing:
    a) stripes
    b) light and dark colors
    c) peroxide
    d) conditioner
    _____

84. Cap, foil, and freehand are techniques for:
    a) blow-drying
    b) conditioning
    c) highlighting
    d) shampooing
    _____

85. Para-phenylenediamine is an ingredient in:
    a) compound dyes
    b) aniline derivative tints
    c) metallic dyes
    d) vegetable tints
    _____

86. Aniline derivative tints are known as:
    a) compound tints
    b) progressive tints
    c) restorer tints
    d) oxidation tints
    _____

87. Aniline derivative tints:
    a) penetrate the hair shaft
    b) harden the hair shaft
    c) coat the hair shaft
    d) none of the above
    _____

88. Aniline derivative tints require a:
    a) special bottle
    b) predisposition test
    c) hot rinse
    d) slow application
    _____

89. When an aniline derivative tint is mixed with hydrogen peroxide, it causes a chemical reaction known as:
    a) presoftening
    b) prelightening
    c) oxidation
    d) blending
    _____

90. Leftover hair tint:
    a) may be boosters
    b) may be used as a lightener
    c) must be discarded
    d) may be used within 10 days ____

91. For permanent color, the color molecules must penetrate into the:
    a) cuticle
    b) follicle
    c) medulla
    d) cortex ____

92. A single-application tint is prepared by mixing the required tints with:
    a) distilled water
    b) hydrogen peroxide
    c) ammonia water
    d) certified color ____

93. The more lift a haircolor has, the less color it is able to:
    a) deposit
    b) remove
    c) correct
    d) bleach ____

94. Lift and deposit can be adjusted by:
    a) adding tint
    b) varying peroxide volume
    c) adding bleach
    d) varying brands ____

95. Mix hair tint with the developer in a/an:
    a) neutralizer bottle
    b) glass or plastic bowl
    c) aluminum bowl
    d) paper cup ____

96. Before applying a one-process tint, the client must be given a:
    a) preshampoo
    b) patch test
    c) presoftener
    d) prelightener ____

97. Body heat and incomplete keratinization make color process faster at the:
    a) ends
    b) midshaft
    c) kernels
    d) scalp ____

98. In a retouch, the hair tint is first applied to the:
    a) hair ends
    b) entire hair shaft
    c) new growth
    d) hairline only ____

99. To avoid overlapping in a tint retouch, color the new growth of the hair:
    a) $\frac{1}{16}$th of an inch over tinted hair
    b) up to the tinted hair
    c) $\frac{1}{4}$th of an inch over the tinted hair
    d) $\frac{1}{2}$ of an inch over the tinted hair ____

100. To change the color of a client's hair to a much lighter shade, the hair colorist should do what to the hair?
    a) presoften it
    b) prelighten it
    c) tone it
    d) neutralize it ____

101. What a preliminary action should be taken when the hair is gray and resistant?
    a) it should be colored twice
    b) it should be color-blended
    c) it should be presoftened
    d) it should be preshaped ____

102. Presoftening before applying a double-process hair tint serves to:
    a) remove metallic dye
    b) increase elasticity
    c) harden lightened hair
    d) increase porosity
    ____

103. Presoftening also creates missing yellow or gold tones so tint will:
    a) be pale blonde
    b) process on-tone
    c) look brassy
    d) not be needed
    ____

104. Special preparations that equalize porosity and deposit base color in one application are called:
    a) spacers
    b) single-process tints
    c) fillers
    d) two-step tints
    ____

105. Porous areas of the hair are prevented from absorbing too much tint by the application of a:
    a) filler
    b) presoftener
    c) toner
    d) color rinse
    ____

106. A base color that is deposited on damaged hair in order to take and hold color evenly is a/an:
    a) color filler
    b) rinse
    c) developer
    d) oxidizer
    ____

107. Two types of fillers are color fillers and:
    a) cream fillers
    b) toner fillers
    c) conditioning fillers
    d) process fillers
    ____

108. Conditioner and color fillers are recommended for:
    a) virgin hair
    b) hairpieces
    c) damaged hair
    d) oily hair
    ____

109. A correctly selected color filler replaces the _____ in the color formulations.
    a) missing primary
    b) missing secondary
    c) complementary
    d) missing tertiary
    ____

110. To correct faded color, first identify:
    a) manufacturer
    b) home-care products
    c) cause of fading
    d) vitamin overdose
    ____

111. Scarves, hats, air drying, and lower volume peroxide are all ways to prevent:
    a) fading
    b) salon visits
    c) seeing mistakes
    d) sunburn
    ____

112. Excessive brassiness can be camouflaged by applying:
    a) conditioner
    b) complementary color
    c) brass remover
    d) touch-ups
    ____

113. Color removers are designed to:
    a) strip conditioners
    b) correct porosity
    c) diffuse pigment
    d) shampoo in
    ____

114. Color removers are usually followed by:
    a) double-application color
    c) blonde toners
    b) bleach
    d) perms ——

115. Tinting lightened hair to its natural shade is known as a:
    a) prelightener
    c) presoftener
    b) stripper
    d) tint back ——

116. Most salon color services are performed to:
    a) correct home mistakes
    c) keep staff busy
    b) cover or enhance
    d) use leftover product ——

117. Smoking and medication can cause gray hair to:
    a) fall out
    c) turn blue
    b) whiten
    d) yellow ——

Chemical Hair Relaxing and Soft-curl Permanent

1. The process of straightening overcurly hair by the use of chemical agents is known as chemical hair:
   a) neutralizing
   b) stabilizing
   c) relaxing
   d) stranding   ____

2. The action of the chemical relaxer causes the hair to:
   a) soften and swell
   b) form new curls
   c) harden and set
   d) shrink   ____

3. What chemical is often required in addition to the chemical relaxer?
   a) gel
   b) processing time
   c) waving lotion
   d) stabilizer   ____

4. To predetermine the results of a chemical relaxing treatment, it may be necessary to take a:
   a) patch test
   b) stabilizing test
   c) filler test
   d) strand test   ____

5. If the hair is damaged due to hot-comb straightening, tinting, or lightening, the cosmetologist should:
   a) give the relaxer, then condition
   b) refuse the relaxer until conditioning treatments are given
   c) give the relaxer, then retint
   d) retint the hair, then give the relaxer   ____

6. A factor that affects processing time of the chemical relaxer is:
   a) age of client
   b) hair filler
   c) hair color
   d) hair porosity   ____

7. The scalp and skin are protected from possible burns when using a hair relaxer by applying:
   a) violet jelly
   b) stabilizer
   c) sodium hydroxide
   d) base   ____

8. After the hair has been processed with a sodium hydroxide relaxer and before the shampoo, the hair should be thoroughly:
   a) brushed
   b) rinsed
   c) combed
   d) conditioned   ____

9. Before applying a thio relaxer, the hair should be:
   a) comb pressed
   b) vigorously brushed
   c) stabilized
   d) shampooed   ____

10. The relaxer cream is applied last near the scalp because processing is increased in this area by:
    a) the accelerator
    b) 10% ammonia
    c) body heat
    d) hydrogen peroxide   ____

11. Combing tangles roughly from the hair after a chemical relaxing treatment may cause hair:
a) reversion
b) breakage
c) discoloration
d) strengthening
_____

12. The test that determines the hair's degree of elasticity is known as the _____ test.
a) finger
b) match
c) pull
d) relaxer
_____

13. The best type of shampoo to use after the chemical relaxer is a/an:
a) organic
b) nonalkaline
c) toning
d) alkaline
_____

14. After a chemical relaxing treatment, a hair conditioner is applied:
a) before styling the hair
b) after styling the hair
c) after the hair is dried
d) before combing the set
_____

15. When analyzing hair condition, it is necessary to evaluate the hair's porosity, texture, and:
a) style
b) color
c) cut
d) elasticity
_____

16. The two commonly used methods of chemical hair relaxing are the thio method and the _____ method.
a) thermal
b) sodium hydroxide
c) single-process
d) double-process
_____

17. A hair relaxing treatment should be avoided when an examination shows the presence of scalp:
a) looseness
b) abrasions
c) tightness
d) flexibility
_____

18. Hair porosity refers to the ability of the hair to:
a) color evenly
b) resist service
c) stretch and return
d) absorb moisture
_____

19. Hair elasticity refers to the ability of the hair to:
a) repel moisture
b) stretch and return
c) absorb moisture
d) resist service
_____

20. Hair texture refers to the degree of the hair's coarseness or:
a) fineness
b) absorption
c) flexibility
d) elasticity
_____

21. A blowout style is a combination of hairstyling and chemical hair:
a) coloring
b) perming
c) straightening
d) designing
_____

22. The chemical blowout may be done with either thio or:
a) hot thermal iron
b) neutralizer
c) sodium hydroxide
d) fixative or stabilizer
_____

23. When performing a chemical blowout, the important consideration is that the hair must *not* be:
   a) air waved
   b) overrelaxed
   c) underrelaxed
   d) lifted ___

24. The natural oils removed by the relaxer are replaced by:
   a) shampooing
   b) stabilizing
   c) rinsing
   d) conditioning ___

25. Soft-curl permanent waving is a method of:
   a) permanent-waving straight hair
   b) permanent-waving overcurly hair
   c) permanently relaxing the hair
   d) relaxing permanent-waved hair ___

26. A soft-curl permanent should *not* be given to hair that is:
   a) relaxed with sodium hydroxide
   b) not chemically relaxed
   c) relaxed with ammonium thioglycolate
   d) longer than 4 inches ___

27. Thio gel or cream, used in giving a soft-curl perm, is applied to the hair in order to:
   a) harden the hair after processing
   b) harden the hair before processing
   c) soften the hair for wrapping
   d) soften the hair for styling ___

28. In order to arrange the curl pattern, the rods selected for a soft-curl permanent should be:
   a) at least 2 times larger than natural curl
   b) one size smaller than natural curl
   c) equal to the natural curl
   d) at least 2 times larger than desired curl ___

29. In order to achieve good curl formation, the hair should circle the rod at least:
   a) 2½ times
   b) 4 times
   c) 1½ times
   d) 1 time ___

30. When giving a soft-curl perm, apply thio until all hair on rods is thoroughly saturated, then:
   a) resaturate each rod
   b) rinse excess thio
   c) replace saturated cotton
   d) remove rods carefully ___

31. After properly neutralizing a soft-curl perm, it is important to:
   a) remove rods carefully
   b) rinse with hot water
   c) leave hair on rods until dry
   d) apply presoftener ___

32. When giving a soft-curl perm, the hair is most often cut:
   a) before processing
   b) after neutralizing
   c) before neutralizing
   d) three weeks after service ___

Thermal Hair Straightening

1. Comb pressing with heat is commonly referred to as a:
   a) marcel press   c) croquignole press
   b) deep press   d) soft press   ___

2. The temperature of the pressing comb should be adjusted to the hair's:
   a) cleanliness   c) texture
   b) shortness   d) length   ___

3. The best time to give a hair press is:
   a) before a shampoo   c) before styling
   b) after a shampoo   d) after a hair styling ___

4. The least difficult type of hair for you to give a hair press is:
   a) very wiry, curly hair   c) hair with compact cuticle
   b) very resistant, curly hair d) medium curly hair   ___

5. When pressing gray hair, use light pressure and:
   a) more heat   c) intense heat
   b) moderate heat   d) a and c   ___

6. Hair that appears lifeless and limp is usually lacking in:
   a) elasticity   c) porosity
   b) texture   d) density   ___

7. The type of hair that requires the least heat and pressure is:
   a) coarse   c) medium, curly
   b) fine   d) curly   ___

8. It is not advisable to press the client's hair if the following condition is present:
   a) hair dryness   c) scalp injury
   b) hair oiliness   d) dandruff   ___

9. A double treatment with a heated comb is known as a:
   a) soft press   c) regular press
   b) hard press   d) comb press   ___

10. Hair pressing:
    a) permanently waves   c) temporarily straightens
       the hair   overcurly hair
    b) temporarily curls   d) gives wide waves
       straight hair   to curly hair   ___

11. A good hair-pressing treatment:
    a) improves hair texture c) improves hair condition
    b) is not harmful to hair d) is harmful to the scalp ___

12. A press is given with:
    a) marcel irons   c) cold-wave lotion
    b) a pressing comb   d) permanent-wave lotion ___

13. If the pressing comb is not hot enough, the hair:
    a) will straighten easily   c) will turn lighter
    b) will not straighten   d) will become dry   ____

14. Burnt hair strands:
    a) can be reconditioned   c) can be made oily
    b) cannot be reconditioned d) grow more rapidly   ____

15. In pressing coarse hair, more heat is required because:
    a) it contains no medulla   c) it has no cuticle
    b) it has the greatest   d) it has the smallest
       diameter   diameter   ____

16. When giving a hair press to coarse, overcurly hair, it can tolerate:
    a) less heat than fine hair   c) less pressing oil
    b) less pressure than   d) more heat and pressure
       medium hair   than fine hair   ____

17. To avoid breakage when pressing fine hair, the following is required:
    a) more heat and pressure c) a stronger chemical lotion
    b) less heat and pressure   d) no pressing oil   ____

18. The use of excess heat on gray, tinted, or lightened hair may:
    a) make the hair appear oily c) discolor the hair
    b) make the hair wiry   d) add moisture to the hair   ____

19. Failure to correct dry and brittle hair before thermal straightening may result in:
    a) hair breakage   c) hair relaxing
    b) deep waves   d) over curling   ____

20. To avoid smoke or burning while pressing hair, use:
    a) more heat   c) less pressing oil
    b) preheated pressing oil   d) more pressing oil   ____

21. Hard press also is known as a:
    a) chemical press   c) thermal press
    b) double press   d) rod press   ____

22. Hair pressing treatments between shampoos are called:
    a) touch-ups   c) scalp treatments
    b) reconditioning treatments d) patch tests   ____

23. When pressing lightened or tinted hair, use light pressure and:
    a) more heat   c) intense heat
    b) moderate heat   d) no heat   ____

24. Wiry, overcurly hair has qualities that make it:
    a) easy to press   c) impossible to press
    b) difficult to press   d) normal to press   ____

25. Damaged hair contains:
    a) considerable elasticity c) considerable oil
    b) little or no elasticity   d) an extra large medulla   ____

26. A scalp may be classified as normal, flexible, or:
    a) brittle
    c) porous
    b) elastic
    d) tight ____

27. In examining the client's hair and scalp, the cosmetologist should look for:
    a) liver spots on the scalp
    c) moles behind the ears
    b) freckles on the forehead
    d) abrasions on the scalp ____

28. Pressing combs should be constructed of good quality steel or:
    a) zinc
    c) plastic
    b) hard rubber
    d) brass ____

29. The actual pressing or straightening of the hair is accomplished with the comb's:
    a) teeth
    c) back rod
    b) handle
    d) litmus ____

30. Hair and scalp may be reconditioned with special hair products, hair brushing, and:
    a) hair pressing treatments
    c) a lemon rinse
    b) scalp massage
    d) a dry shampoo ____

31. A tight scalp can be made more flexible by hair brushing and:
    a) cold-water rinses
    c) scalp massage
    b) a soft press
    d) liquid dry shampoo ____

32. When giving a pressing treatment, the cosmetologist should avoid:
    a) excessive heat and pressure
    c) pressing oil
    b) thoroughly drying the hair
    d) uniform sectioning of hair ____

33. Too frequent hair-pressing treatments can cause:
    a) excessive oiliness of hair
    c) progressive hair breakage
    b) hirsuties
    d) hypertrichosis ____

34. The pressing comb is kept clean by rubbing its outside surface and between its teeth with an emery board, fine steel wood, or fine sand paper, which removes:
    a) hair
    c) grease
    b) carbon
    d) dust ____

The Artistry of Artificial Hair

1. When styling a wig, pin curls are used in certain areas of the head instead of rollers to keep the:
   a) fibers from unraveling
   b) fullness of the style
   c) style close to the head
   d) hair tightly knotted _____

2. Human hair wigs may be colored with a color rinse that lasts:
   a) permanently
   b) six months
   c) only a few days
   d) from cleaning to cleaning _____

3. Human hair wigs can be distinguished from synthetic hair wigs by a simple:
   a) tinting test
   b) match test
   c) predisposition test
   d) strand test _____

4. Human hair wigs may be properly cleaned by:
   a) a liquid cleaning
   b) a shampoo tint
   c) an alkaline soap
   d) sodium hydroxide _____

5. If wigs are worn frequently, they should be cleaned every:
   a) 2–4 weeks
   b) 8–10 weeks
   c) 2–3 months
   d) 4–6 months _____

6. Dryness or brittleness of wigs is prevented by:
   a) permanent waving
   b) drycleaning
   c) conditioning
   d) dry shampooing _____

7. A wig or hairpiece made of human hair should *never* be:
   a) drycleaned
   b) lightened
   c) color rinsed
   d) shaped _____

8. A long weft of hair mounted with a loop at the end is known as a:
   a) wig
   b) bandeau
   c) switch
   d) wiglet _____

9. A wiglet is used primarily to blend with the client's own hair in order to increase the:
   a) color scheme
   b) casual look
   c) tinting time
   d) amount or density of the hair _____

10. Each time a human hair wig is drycleaned, it should be:
    a) repaired
    b) reconditioned
    c) reknotted
    d) given a hair shaping _____

11. To shorten a wig from front to nape, it is advisable to use:
    a) horizontal tucks
    b) elastic wefts
    c) vertical tucks
    d) horizontal wefts _____

12. To remove width at the back of the wig (from ear to ear), use:
    a) horizontal wefts
    b) elastic wefts
    c) vertical tucks
    d) vertical wefts _____

13. The type of head block that is suitable for all wig services is a:
    a) metal block
    b) porcelain block
    c) canvas block
    d) Styrofoam block _____

Manicuring and Pedicuring

1. Emery boards are used to shape the nail:
   a) side
   b) lunula
   c) free edge
   d) cuticle   ____

2. Nail mend paper is used to:
   a) soften cuticles
   b) repair split nails
   c) remove nail polish
   d) polish the nails   ____

3. Before manicuring implements are used, they should be:
   a) wiped with a tissue
   b) wiped with a towel
   c) cleansed and sanitized
   d) dipped in warm water   ____

4. Brittle nails and dry cuticles are treated with a/an:
   a) oil manicure
   b) top sealer
   c) regular manicure
   d) machine manicure   ____

5. Sanitized manicuring implements should be stored:
   a) in a table drawer
   b) in an open cabinet
   c) in a cabinet sanitizer
   d) on the manicuring table   ____

6. Manicuring implements should be sanitized:
   a) once a day
   b) after each use
   c) every week
   d) twice a week   ____

7. A manicure that is not given in the manicuring area, and is often given while the client is receiving another service is called a/an _____ manicure.
   a) booth
   b) hot oil
   c) plain
   d) artificial   ____

8. While a manicure is being given, instruments should be kept in a/an:
   a) manicuring table drawer
   b) alcohol jar sanitizer
   c) finger bowl
   d) manicurist's pocket   ____

9. To help prevent dry skin around the nails, apply:
   a) cuticle cream
   b) nail polish remover
   c) alcohol
   d) an antiseptic   ____

10. When shaping the fingernail, the nail is filed from:
    a) corner to center
    b) straight across
    c) center to corner
    d) corner to corner   ____

11. The instrument used for trimming the cuticle is a:
    a) buffer
    b) pusher
    c) nipper
    d) brush   ____

12. A cosmetic used to correct a dry cuticle is cuticle:
    a) cream
    b) whitener
    c) abrasive
    d) solvent   ____

13. The correct way to apply nail polish from base to free edge is to:
    a) use thick polish
    b) use short, jerky strokes
    c) apply three coats
    d) apply it quickly and lightly ____

14. A cosmetic applied over the nail polish to minimize chipping or cracking is a/an:
    a) base coat
    b) seal coat
    c) lacquer
    d) abrasive ____

15. To remove old nail polish from the nails, use:
    a) olive oil
    b) peroxide
    c) polish remover
    d) liquid soap ____

16. Apply nail polish:
    a) over the top coat
    b) over the base coat
    c) over the sealer
    d) before the base coat ____

17. The ideal nail shape is:
    a) tapered
    b) rectangular
    c) oval
    d) round ____

18. For a more natural effect, the shape of the nails should conform to the:
    a) hands
    b) cuticle
    c) skin texture
    d) fingertips ____

19. Wavy ridges may be improved by buffing the nail with:
    a) pumice powder
    b) cream
    c) oil
    d) polish remover ____

20. Artificial nails help to:
    a) lengthen nails
    b) cover up an infection
    c) make nails grow faster
    d) prevent nail discoloration ____

21. A nail buffer must not be used:
    a) with paste polish
    b) with dry polish
    c) where not permitted by law
    d) with pumice polish ____

22. To keep the client's hands flexible, well groomed, and smooth, each manicure should include:
    a) nail wrapping
    b) a pedicure
    c) petrissage
    d) a hand massage ____

23. For clients with ridged and brittle nails or dry cuticles, recommend a/an:
    a) oil manicure
    b) artificial nails
    c) booth manicure
    d) nail wrapping ____

24. The care of the feet, legs, and toenails is called:
    a) pedicuring
    b) hypertrophy
    c) manicuring
    d) paronychia ____

25. What type of nail polish remover should be used on plastic artificial nails?
   a) alcohol
   b) nonalcohol
   c) acetone
   d) nonacetone
   _____

26. Another name for athlete's foot is:
   a) varicose
   b) pityriasis
   c) ringworm
   d) pterygium
   _____

27. To remove stains from nails, use:
   a) nail polish remover
   b) cuticle oil
   c) nail whitener
   d) nail bleach
   _____

28. A stick of nail bleach is wiped:
   a) over the lunula
   b) on top of the free edge
   c) under the free edge
   d) on the sides of the nail
   _____

29. Hand creams and lotions are especially recommended for:
   a) dry, chapped skin
   b) oily skin
   c) tanned skin
   d) freckled skin
   _____

30. The active agent in nail bleach is usually:
   a) water
   b) soap
   c) hydrogen peroxide
   d) detergent
   _____

31. To prevent or correct brittle nails and dry cuticles, use:
   a) nail whitener
   b) cuticle solvent
   c) cuticle cream
   d) dry nail polish
   _____

32. To soften and lubricate the skin around the nails, apply:
   a) pumice powder
   b) nail bleach
   c) cuticle solvent
   d) cuticle oil
   _____

33. Pumice powder is likely to be an ingredient found in a:
   a) cuticle cream
   b) nail abrasive
   c) hand cream
   d) hand lotion
   _____

34. Irregular nail ridges may be smoothed with:
   a) cuticle remover
   b) liquid lacquer
   c) nail solvent
   d) pumice powder
   _____

35. What minimizes the drying effect of the solvent in nail polish remover?
   a) oil
   b) pumice powder
   c) nail whitener
   d) nail bleach
   _____

36. A base coat usually is applied:
   a) over the top coat
   b) after the nail polish
   c) before the nail polish
   d) over the nail polish
   _____

37. A top coat, or sealer, makes the nail polish:
   a) adhere to nail surface
   b) more resistant to chipping
   c) dull in appearance
   d) peel off easily
   _____

38. Soap is to be found in a:
    a) nail white
    b) finger bath
    c) dry nail polish
    d) liquid nail polish   ____

39. To prevent the nails from splitting, apply a nail:
    a) solvent
    b) sealer
    c) strengthener
    d) abrasive   ____

40. The cuticle may be softened with a:
    a) liquid alum
    b) soap bath
    c) sealer
    d) base   ____

41. Nails are protected from chipping by a:
    a) liquid polish
    b) top coat
    c) base coat
    d) powdered alum   ____

42. An adhesive base for liquid nail polish is a:
    a) solvent
    b) sealer
    c) base coat
    d) top coat   ____

The Nail and Its Disorders

1. A healthy nail is smooth, curved, and without hollows or:
   - a) wavy ridges
   - b) flexibility
   - c) firmness
   - d) color
   ____

2. A healthy nail appears to be:
   - a) purplish
   - b) pinkish
   - c) yellowish
   - d) bluish
   ____

3. Nails are appendages of the:
   - a) hair
   - b) oil glands
   - c) sweat glands
   - d) skin
   ____

4. The nail is composed of a substance called:
   - a) melanin
   - b) hemoglobin
   - c) keratin
   - d) corpuscles
   ____

5. In an adult, nails grow at an average of:
   - a) $\frac{1}{8}$" a week
   - b) $\frac{1}{8}$" a month
   - c) $\frac{1}{16}$" a week
   - d) $\frac{1}{16}$" a month
   ____

6. Nails tend to grow faster:
   - a) in the winter
   - b) on elderly people
   - c) on children
   - d) in the spring
   ____

7. The nail plate starts at the nail root and goes to the:
   - a) lunula
   - b) nail matrix
   - c) nail bed
   - d) free edge
   ____

8. The nail root is lodged in the nail mantle at the:
   - a) top of the nail
   - b) base of the nail
   - c) side of the nail
   - d) tip of the nail
   ____

9. The nail root begins from an actively growing tissue called the:
   - a) lunula
   - b) matrix
   - c) hyponychium
   - d) eponychium
   ____

10. The part of the nail that extends over the fingertip is the:
    - a) free edge
    - b) matrix
    - c) nail root
    - d) nail bed
    ____

11. The portion of the skin upon which the nail plate rests is the:
    - a) nail groove
    - b) cuticle
    - c) nail bed
    - d) free edge
    ____

12. Nerves and blood vessels are found in the nail:
    - a) plate
    - b) bed
    - c) lunula
    - d) keratin
    ____

13. The cells of the nail matrix:
    - a) are inactive
    - b) are constantly reproducing
    - c) grow only at night
    - d) undergo a softening process
    ____

14. The lunula is the visible half-moon area at the nail's:
    a) edge
    b) side
    c) base
    d) groove
    ____

15. The lunula of the nail has the shape of a:
    a) full moon
    b) half moon
    c) square
    d) full circle
    ____

16. The cuticle overlapping the lunula is the:
    a) hyponychium
    b) eponychium
    c) mantle
    d) groove
    ____

17. The cuticle is the overlapping skin around the:
    a) finger
    b) nail plate
    c) free edge
    d) none of the above
    ____

18. Nerves and blood vessels are found in the nail:
    a) plate
    b) lunula
    c) matrix
    d) free edge
    ____

19. If the matrix is destroyed, the nail will:
    a) grow back
    b) not grow back
    c) grow faster
    d) grow slower
    ____

20. The overlapping part of the skin around the nail is commonly called the nail:
    a) matrix
    b) groove
    c) mantle
    d) cuticle
    ____

21. The portion of the skin just below the free edge is called the:
    a) hyponychium
    b) eponychium
    c) lunula
    d) nail mantle
    ____

22. The extension of the cuticle skin at the base of the nail is known as the:
    a) hyponychium
    b) mantle
    c) lunula
    d) eponychium
    ____

23. The deep fold of skin in which the nail root is lodged is called the:
    a) mantle
    b) nail groove
    c) nail wall
    d) nail bed
    ____

24. The nail walls are small folds of skin overlapping the sides of the:
    a) mantle
    b) matrix
    c) bed
    d) nail body
    ____

25. The nail grooves are the furrowed tracks at the:
    a) sides of the nail
    b) base of the nail
    c) root of the nail
    d) mantle of the nail
    ____

26. The portion of the cuticle skin that surrounds the entire nail border is the:
    a) mantle
    b) perionychium
    c) nail root
    d) matrix
    ____

27. White spots on the nails are known as:
    a) onychauxis
    b) onychatrophia
    c) leuconychia
    d) hangnails
    ___

28. When the cuticle splits around the nail, it is known as:
    a) onychorrhexis
    b) onychophagy
    c) hangnails
    d) pterygium
    ___

29. Blue nails are usually a sign of:
    a) wrist trouble
    b) stomach ailment
    c) poor blood circulation
    d) lung disorder
    ___

30. Wavy ridges on the nails are caused by:
    a) careless filing of the nails
    b) dryness of the cuticle
    c) uneven growth of the nails
    d) biting the nails
    ___

31. The common name for tinea is:
    a) felon
    b) ingrown nails
    c) ringworm of the nail
    d) brittle nails
    ___

32. Hangnails may be caused by dryness of the:
    a) lunula
    b) dermis
    c) medulla
    d) cuticle
    ___

33. Splitting of the nails may be caused by:
    a) nail polish
    b) careless filing
    c) hangnails
    d) top coat
    ___

34. An infectious and inflammatory condition of the tissues surrounding the nail is known as:
    a) onychatrophia
    b) paronychia
    c) onychia
    d) onychoptosis
    ___

35. Hangnails are treated by softening the cuticle with:
    a) hot oil
    b) boric acid
    c) strong soap
    d) polish remover
    ___

36. Furrows in the nails may be caused by:
    a) an allergy
    b) dermatitis
    c) illness
    d) nail polish
    ___

37. The forward and adhering growth of the cuticle at the base of the nail is called:
    a) atrophy
    b) paronychia
    c) pterygium
    d) onychosis
    ___

38. An infected finger should be treated by a:
    a) manicurist
    b) hairdresser
    c) physician
    d) cosmetologist
    ___

39. The general term for vegetable parasites is:
    a) fungi
    b) spots
    c) onychauxis
    d) matrix
    ___

40. The fungus infection caused when moisture is trapped between the unsanitized natural nail and artifical nail products is called:
    a) spots
    b) fungi
    c) nail mold
    d) bruise
    _____

41. Advanced nail mold causes the nail to turn black and:
    a) harden
    b) smell bad
    c) crumble
    d) split
    _____

42. Onychia is an inflammation with pus formation affecting the:
    a) nail body
    b) nail matrix
    c) free edge
    d) cuticle sides of nail
    _____

43. The technical term indicating any nail disease is:
    a) onychauxis
    b) pterygium
    c) onychosis
    d) leuconychia
    _____

44. If not properly cared for, hangnails may:
    a) become spotted
    b) turn yellow
    c) become infected
    d) become congenital
    _____

45. Furrows may be caused by injury to the cells near the:
    a) free edge
    b) matrix
    c) walls
    d) grooves
    _____

46. Eggshell nails usually are found on persons with a chronic:
    a) digestive disturbance
    b) nervous disturbance
    c) circulatory disturbance
    d) muscular disturbance
    _____

47. An abnormal overgrowth of the nail is known as:
    a) atrophy
    b) hypertrophy
    c) onychophagy
    d) onychorrhexis
    _____

48. The medical term for brittle nails is:
    a) onychorrhexis
    b) onychophagy
    c) hypertrophy
    d) atrophy
    _____

49. The medical term for bitten nails is:
    a) leuconychia
    b) onychia
    c) onychauxis
    d) onychophagy
    _____

Theory of Massage

1. Effleurage, or stroking, is a massage movement applied in a:
   a) heavy tapping manner
   b) deep rolling manner with pressure
   c) light pinching manner
   d) light, slow, and rhythmic manner without firm pressure ____

2. Effleurage is used in massage for its:
   a) stimulating effects
   b) soothing and relaxing effects
   c) invigorating effects
   d) magnetic effects ____

3. Petrissage is what type of massage movement?
   a) friction
   b) percussion
   c) tapotement
   d) kneading ____

4. Petrissage is used in massage for what effects?
   a) soothing
   b) relaxing
   c) invigorating
   d) magnetic ____

5. Friction in massage requires the use of:
   a) vibratory movements
   b) slapping movements
   c) deep rubbing movements
   d) light stroking movements ____

6. Vibration is used in massage for its:
   a) magnetic effects
   b) cooling effects
   c) soothing effects
   d) stimulating effects ____

7. The immediate effects of massage are first noticed:
   a) in the mucous membranes
   b) inside the mouth
   c) on the skin
   d) under the eyelids ____

8. Massage serves to stimulate, tone, and strengthen the:
   a) bone tissue
   b) lymph glands
   c) hair
   d) muscles ____

9. Firm kneading massage movements usually produce what sensation to body tissues?
   a) invigorating
   b) coolness
   c) soothing
   d) relaxing ____

10. Tapotement is what type of massage movement?
    a) vibratory
    b) pinching
    c) friction
    d) tapping ____

11. Massage should not be given when:
    a) freckles are present
    b) albinism is present
    c) abrasions are present
    d) tightness is present ____

12. High blood pressure, heart condition, or stroke are all health conditions that prohibit:
    a) nail mend
    b) massage
    c) nail mold
    d) nail polish ____

Facials

1. The first cream to be used in a plain facial is:
   a) emollient cream
   b) foundation cream
   c) cleansing cream
   d) bleaching cream
   _____

2. When a facial is given, eye pads should be applied before using:
   a) massage manipulations
   b) astringent lotion
   c) foundation cream
   d) infrared light
   _____

3. The sanitized end of a comedone extractor is used to remove:
   a) blackheads
   b) moles
   c) freckles
   d) birthmarks
   _____

4. Following the removal of blackheads, apply to the skin a/an:
   a) deodorant
   b) styptic
   c) astringent
   d) caustic
   _____

5. No face powder or cheek color is applied after giving a/an:
   a) facial for oily skin
   b) facial for dry skin
   c) facial for normal skin
   d) acne treatment
   _____

6. The massage cream used on a dry skin should be a:
   a) cleansing cream
   b) lubricating cream
   c) cold cream
   d) pumice cream
   _____

7. After the massage cream has been removed, the face should be sponged with a/an:
   a) caustic lotion
   b) disinfectant lotion
   c) setting lotion
   d) astringent lotion
   _____

8. What does negative galvanic current used during a facial do to the skin?
   a) closes the pores
   b) dries the skin
   c) opens the pores
   d) removes comedones
   _____

9. A hot oil mask should be recommended for:
   a) oily skin
   b) dry skin
   c) aging skin
   d) bleaching freckles
   _____

10. Dry skin may be caused by underactive:
    a) sudoriferous glands
    b) thyroid glands
    c) sebaceous glands
    d) salivary glands
    _____

11. When skillfully applied, massage benefits the skin by:
    a) increasing tension
    b) deep cleansing
    c) removing milia
    d) stimulation
    _____

12. For dry skin, avoid using lotions that contain a large percentage of:
    a) lanolin
    b) hormones
    c) alcohol
    d) oil
    _____

13. When receiving a facial, an important part for the client is:
    a) tension
    b) relaxation
    c) conversation
    d) stimulation
    _____

14. Overactive sebaceous glands produce too much:
    a) sebum
    b) perspiration
    c) moisture
    d) milia
    _____

15. The direction of pressure in facial massage movements should be from the muscle:
    a) origin to insertion
    b) insertion to origin
    c) posterior to inferior
    d) superior to inferior
    _____

16. When received as a regular service, facials result in improved skin tone and improved:
    a) density
    b) texture
    c) porosity
    d) moles
    _____

17. Studies show that acne may be due to:
    a) extreme cleanliness
    b) lack of skin treatments
    c) balanced diet
    d) hereditary factors
    _____

18. Sebaceous blackheads are caused by a hardened mass of sebum in the ducts of the:
    a) thyroid glands
    b) salivary glands
    c) sebaceous glands
    d) sudoriferous glands
    _____

19. Milia is a common skin disorder that often occurs in skin texture that is:
    a) coarse
    b) flabby
    c) fine
    d) dry
    _____

20. Facial treatments are given either for skin correction or:
    a) coloration
    b) preservation
    c) endocrination
    d) digestion
    _____

21. Acne is found to be a disorder of the:
    a) sudoriferous glands
    b) thyroid glands
    c) sebaceous glands
    d) salivary glands
    _____

22. An egg facial mask will cleanse the pores and:
    a) lubricate the skin
    b) remove wrinkles
    c) cover freckles
    d) tighten the skin
    _____

Facial Makeup

1. Makeup is applied to the face for the purpose of:
   a) correcting an oily skin
   b) darkening natural coloring
   c) lubricating the skin
   d) improving its appearance ___

2. Cream and liquid foundations are formulated for both oily and _____ skins.
   a) whitehead
   b) blackhead
   c) acne
   d) dry ___

3. Face powder should:
   a) be darker than the foundation
   b) blend with the color tone of skin
   c) be lighter than the foundation
   d) be eliminated when using foundation ___

4. Cheek color (rouge) should be:
   a) less vivid in daylight than at night
   b) three shades lighter than lip color
   c) darker than lip color
   d) all of the above ___

5. In corrective makeup a lighter shade is used to:
   a) minimize a facial area
   b) produce a shadow effect
   c) conceal blemishes
   d) emphasize a facial area ___

6. In corrective makeup, a darker shade is used to:
   a) emphasize a facial area
   b) minimize a facial area
   c) highlight a facial area
   d) conceal blemishes ___

7. The color of foundation is tested by blending on the patron's:
   a) jawline
   b) eyelids
   c) forehead
   d) wrist ___

8. Lipcolor (lipstick) should:
   a) match nail and cheek colors
   b) coordinate with cheek color
   c) be the same color as a costume color
   d) a and c ___

9. The primary objective of corrective makeup is to create an optical illusion of a/an:
   a) oval face
   b) diamond-shaped face
   c) round face
   d) heart-shaped face ___

10. In corrective makeup, use a lighter shade than the foundation to:
    a) decrease the size of features
    b) produce a shadow effect
    c) make prominent features less noticeable
    d) produce a highlight effect ___

11. In corrective makeup, use a foundation that is darker than the original one to:
    a) produce a highlight effect
    b) produce a shadow effect
    c) produce no effect
    d) make prominent features more noticeable _____

12. To make the eyes look larger and lashes appear thicker, apply:
    a) eye shadow
    b) eye cream
    c) eyeliners
    d) cheek color _____

13. The application of foundation cream helps to conceal:
    a) eyes
    b) highlights
    c) wrinkles
    d) lightening _____

14. Eyebrows should be properly tweezed in the direction:
    a) opposite to their natural growth
    b) of their natural growth
    c) toward the chin
    d) toward the scalp _____

15. Applying hot cotton on the eyebrows before tweezing tends to:
    a) make it more painful
    b) soften and relax eyebrows
    c) tighten the tissues
    d) contract the skin _____

16. An astringent lotion is applied after tweezing the eyebrows in order to:
    a) relax the skin
    b) contract the skin
    c) expand the skin
    d) stimulate the skin _____

17. To remove stray hair from above the brow use a:
    a) depilatory
    b) electric clipper
    c) tweezer
    d) safety razor _____

18. To minimize wide-set eyes and make them appear closer, it is best to:
    a) shorten the outside eyebrow line on both sides
    b) extend the eyebrow line to inside the corner of the eye
    c) make the eyebrow line straight
    d) arch the ends of the eyebrow _____

19. To minimize close-set eyes, space the brows to:
    a) widen the distance between them
    b) shorten the distance between them
    c) shorten the browline to the end of the eye
    d) extend the browline beyond the outside corner of the eye _____

20. To help avoid infection during eyebrow arching, apply a/an:
    a) disinfectant
    b) antiseptic
    c) deodorant
    d) powder _____

21. The process of affixing semipermanent individual eyelashes is referred to as:
    a) stripping
    b) eye tabbing
    c) adhesive lashes
    d) brush lashes
    _____

22. Semipermanent individual eyelashes are made of:
    a) human hair
    b) feather fibers
    c) adhesive fibers
    d) synthetic fibers
    _____

23. Semipermanent individual eyelashes last for a period of:
    a) 6–8 weeks
    b) 3–6 months
    c) 2–3 weeks
    d) 15–20 weeks
    _____

24. Individual semipermanent eyelashes are attached to the client's:
    a) temples
    b) eyelashes
    c) eyebrows
    d) bridge of nose
    _____

25. Before applying individual lashes, it is advisable to give a/an:
    a) color test
    b) endurance test
    c) strand test
    d) allergy test
    _____

26. For a more natural look, strip eyelashes should be:
    a) shortened
    b) very long
    c) lightened
    d) feathered
    _____

27. The individual lashes will not stay on as long on the lower eyelids because of the abundance of:
    a) natural oils
    b) perspiration
    c) respiration
    d) salivary glands
    _____

28. False eyelashes will not hold as long on clients with:
    a) sparse eyelashes
    b) cemented eyelashes
    c) eye tabbing
    d) oily eyelids
    _____

29. Clients with gaps between their eyelashes are said to have:
    a) tabbed eyelashes
    b) luxurious eyelashes
    c) sparse eyelashes
    d) strip eyelashes
    _____

30. In addition to eye tabbing, another type of false eyelashes is:
    a) individual eyelashes
    b) strip lashes
    c) semipermanent lashes
    d) adhesive lashes
    _____

The Skin and Its Disorders

1. The largest organ of the human body is the:
   a) heart
   b) lungs
   c) skin
   d) stomach   ____

2. A healthy skin should be:
   a) perfectly dry
   b) without any color
   c) slightly moist and soft
   d) bluish in color   ____

3. A good complexion is an indication of the skin's fine texture and:
   a) pale color
   b) healthy color
   c) dry condition
   d) bluish color   ____

4. The skin is thinnest on the:
   a) eyebrows
   b) eyelids
   c) forehead
   d) backs of the hands   ____

5. The skin is thickest on the:
   a) palms and soles
   b) cheeks
   c) forehead
   d) chin   ____

6. The two main divisions of the skin are the epidermis and:
   a) subcutaneous tissue
   b) dermis
   c) corneum layer
   d) melanin   ____

7. The outer protective layer of the skin is called the:
   a) dermis
   b) adipose tissue
   c) epidermis
   d) subcutaneous tissue   ____

8. No blood vessels are to be found in the:
   a) dermis
   b) cutis
   c) subcutis
   d) epidermis   ____

9. Blood vessels, nerves, and sweat and oil glands are found in the:
   a) epidermis
   b) dermis
   c) cuticle layer
   d) scarf layer   ____

10. The color of the skin depends on the blood supply to the skin and the coloring pigment called:
    a) keratin
    b) melanin
    c) fat
    d) moisture   ____

11. The layer of the epidermis that is continually being shed and replaced is the:
    a) stratum lucidum
    b) stratum corneum
    c) stratum granulosum
    d) stratum mucosum   ____

12. Stratum corneum is also known as the:
    a) clear layer
    b) horny layer
    c) granular layer
    d) basal layer   ____

13. Over a long period of time, continued pressure and friction on the skin will cause an area to become:
    a) slippery
    b) thinner
    c) callused
    d) scaly
    ___

14. The epidermis contains many:
    a) blood vessels
    b) small nerve endings
    c) adipose tissues
    d) subcutaneous tissues
    ___

15. Keratin (a protein substance in the epidermis) is found in the:
    a) stratum mucosum
    b) stratum corneum
    c) stratum lucidum
    d) stratum granulosum
    ___

16. The stratum corneum is the outermost layer of the:
    a) dermis
    b) true skin
    c) epidermis
    d) corium
    ___

17. The stratum germinativum is the innermost layer of the:
    a) dermis
    b) epidermis
    c) subcutaneous tissue
    d) corium
    ___

18. The growth of the epidermis starts in the stratum:
    a) lucidum
    b) germinativum
    c) corneum
    d) granulosum
    ___

19. The dermis is also known as the corium, cutis, derma, or:
    a) cuticle
    b) true skin
    c) false skin
    d) fatty tissue
    ___

20. The reticular and papillary layers are found in the:
    a) epidermis
    b) dermis
    c) cuticle
    d) adipose tissue
    ___

21. The papillary layer of the dermis contains looped capillaries and:
    a) adipose tissue
    b) hair papillae
    c) subcutaneous tissue
    d) tactile corpuscles
    ___

22. The reticular layer is the inner portion of the:
    a) epidermis
    b) dermis
    c) cuticle
    d) subcutis
    ___

23. Subcutaneous tissue consists mainly of:
    a) muscle tissue
    b) fatty cells
    c) keratin
    d) pigment
    ___

24. Sensory nerve fibers in the skin react to:
    a) hair follicles
    b) freckles
    c) skin pigment
    d) touch
    ___

25. Melanin is found in the stratum germinativum and:
    a) stratum corneum
    b) adipose tissue
    c) papillary layer
    d) reticular layer
    ___

26. Melanin protects the skin from the harmful action of:
    a) bacteria
    c) ultraviolet rays
    b) pressure
    d) electrical current   _____

27. Skin elasticity is due to the presence of elastic tissue in the:
    a) dermis
    c) subcutaneous tissue
    b) epidermis
    d) cuticle   _____

28. The sebaceous glands secrete:
    a) melanin
    c) sebum
    b) saliva
    d) perspiration   _____

29. The function of sebum is to keep the skin:
    a) clean
    c) dry
    b) lubricated
    d) hard   _____

30. The skin is lubricated by an oily substance known as:
    a) sweat
    c) hormone
    b) sebum
    d) enzyme   _____

31. The duct of an oil gland empties into the:
    a) blood vessel
    c) sweat pore
    b) hair follicle
    d) hair papilla   _____

32. No oil glands are found on the:
    a) palms
    c) forehead
    b) face
    d) scalp   _____

33. The sweat glands of the skin excrete:
    a) sebum
    c) an oily substance
    b) perspiration
    d) oxygen   _____

34. The sweat glands help to eliminate one of the following from the body:
    a) oxygen
    c) oil
    b) waste products
    d) sebum   _____

35. The small openings of the sweat glands on the skin are called:
    a) follicles
    c) pores
    b) capillaries
    d) papillae   _____

36. The sweat and oil glands are known as:
    a) ductless glands
    c) duct glands
    b) endocrine glands
    d) sensory glands   _____

37. The excretion of perspiration from the skin is under the control of the:
    a) muscular system
    c) respiratory system
    b) circulatory system
    d) nervous system   _____

38. The blood and sweat glands of the skin regulate body heat by maintaining a Fahrenheit temperature of about:
    a) 50°
    c) 150°
    b) 75°
    d) 98.6°   _____

39. The skin responds to heat, cold, and touch because of its:
    a) blood supply   c) lymph supply
    b) nerve supply   d) sweat and oil glands   ___

40. The palms, soles, forehead, and armpits contain an abundance of:
    a) salivary glands   c) sweat glands
    b) gastric glands   d) adrenal glands   ___

41. Endings of nerve fibers in the papillary layer are called:
    a) white corpuscles   c) tactile corpuscles
    b) erythrocytes   d) red corpuscles   ___

42. The activity of the sweat glands is increased by:
    a) cold   c) rest
    b) heat   d) sleep   ___

43. Of the following skin structures, the most active in temperature regulation are the:
    a) follicle glands   c) sweat glands
    b) sebaceous glands   d) oil glands   ___

44. The ability of the skin to stretch and regain its natural shape reveals its:
    a) tension   c) dryness
    b) oiliness   d) pliability   ___

45. The subcutaneous tissue is:
    a) above the cuticle   c) below the dermis
    b) above the epidermis   d) below the adipose   ___

46. Motor nerve fibers are distributed to the:
    a) sweat glands   c) epidermis
    b) oil glands   d) arrector pili muscles   ___

47. The adipose tissue gives the skin its:
    a) contour   c) color
    b) pliability   d) sensation   ___

48. Secretory nerve fibers of the skin are distributed to the:
    a) blood vessels   c) lymph glands
    b) ganglia vessels   d) sweat and oil glands   ___

49. Structures that are appendages to the skin are hair, sweat glands, oil glands, and:
    a) motor fibers   c) blood vessels
    b) nails   d) sensory fibers   ___

50. The skin is nourished by:
    a) watery fluids   c) body gases
    b) blood and lymph   d) chemical solutions   ___

51. Dermatology deals with the structure, functions, and disorders of the:
    a) nails   c) hair
    b) bones   d) skin   ___

52. Trichology deals with the study and disorders of the:
  a) skin
  b) hair
  c) nails
  d) bones
  _____

53. Pathology deals with the study of:
  a) normal body functions
  b) normal body structures
  c) disease
  d) normal body changes
  _____

54. Symptoms are outward signs revealing:
  a) normal body functions
  b) indications of disease
  c) body coordination
  d) normal body changes
  _____

55. If a client has a skin disease, the cosmetologist should:
  a) treat it with medicine
  b) overlook it
  c) refer client to a physician
  d) suggest self-treatment
  _____

56. Itching is an example of a/an:
  a) subjective symptom
  b) objective symptom
  c) primary skin lesion
  d) secondary skin lesion
  _____

57. A papule is a:
  a) secondary skin lesion
  b) primary skin lesion
  c) tertiary skin lesion
  d) subjective symptom
  _____

58. Pus is most likely to be found in:
  a) vesicles
  b) scars
  c) macules
  d) pustules
  _____

59. Another name for a vesicle is a/an:
  a) cicatrix
  b) abrasion
  c) blister
  d) scab
  _____

60. The skin lesion found in chapped lips and hands is called a:
  a) fissure
  b) papule
  c) stain
  d) tumor
  _____

61. After a wound heals, a/an _____ develops.
  a) infection
  b) scar
  c) carbuncle
  d) furuncle
  _____

62. An abnormal cell mass is known as a:
  a) papule
  b) macule
  c) tumor
  d) pustule
  _____

63. A disease lasting a long time is described as:
  a) chronic
  b) acute
  c) objective
  d) subjective
  _____

64. A disease lasting a short time is described as:
  a) acute
  b) chronic
  c) congenital
  d) occupational
  _____

65. An open skin lesion containing pus is known as a/an:
  a) papule
  b) bulla
  c) ulcer
  d) fissure
  _____

66. A disease that spreads by personal contact is known as a:
    a) non-contagious disease   c) contagious disease
    b) systemic disease   d) deficiency disease   ____

67. A disease that attacks a large number of people in a particular location is known as a/an:
    a) constitutional disease   c) epidemic
    b) systemic disease   d) non-contagious disease   ____

68. Comedone is the technical name for a:
    a) whitehead   c) blackhead
    b) pimple   d) dry skin   ____

69. Milia is the technical name for:
    a) whiteheads   c) pimples
    b) blackheads   d) dry skin   ____

70. Acne is a disorder of the:
    a) sweat glands   c) intestinal glands
    b) sebaceous glands   d) stomach glands   ____

71. Acne, or common pimple, is known as acne simplex or acne:
    a) rosacea   c) vulgaris
    b) seborrhea   d) steatoma   ____

72. One of the symptoms of asteatosis is a/an:
    a) oily skin   c) dry skin
    b) itchy skin   d) warm skin   ____

73. In seborrhea, the appearance of the skin is:
    a) dry and dull   c) oily and shiny
    b) scaly   d) red blotched   ____

74. Acne is indicated on the face by the presence of:
    a) wheals   c) whiteheads
    b) pimples   d) blackheads   ____

75. Comedones and pimples occur mostly among:
    a) infants   c) younger people
    b) adults   d) older people   ____

76. Steatoma is indicated by the presence of a sebaceous cyst on:
    a) face   c) legs
    b) arms   d) scalp, neck, and back   ____

77. Excessive oiliness of the hair is caused by over-activity of the:
    a) arrector pili   c) sweat glands
    b) stomach glands   d) sebaceous glands   ____

78. An oil scalp is usually caused by:
    a) insufficient brushing   c) over-active sebaceous glands
    b) frequent shampooing   d) thorough rinsing   ____

79. Bromidrosis means:
    a) lack of perspiration   c) excessive perspiration
    b) foul smelling perspiration d) discolored perspiration ____

80. Excessive perspiration is:
   a) anhidrosis
   b) osmidrosis
   c) hyperhidrosis
   d) bromidrosis
   ____

81. Anhidrosis means:
   a) lack of perspiration
   b) excessive perspiration
   c) foul-smelling perspiration
   d) prickly heat
   ____

82. People exposed to excessive heat may develop a condition known as:
   a) anhidrosis
   b) chromidrosis
   c) hemidrosis
   d) hyperhidrosis
   ____

83. Prickly heat is also known as:
   a) military fever
   b) miliaria rubra
   c) herpes simplex
   d) steatoma
   ____

84. Hyperhidrosis occurs most frequently in the area of the:
   a) elbows
   b) armpits
   c) ankles
   d) wrists
   ____

85. The term meaning inflammation is:
   a) alopecia
   b) dermatitis
   c) canities
   d) lentigo
   ____

86. Certain chemicals found in cosmetics may cause dermatitis:
   a) simplex
   b) venenata
   c) seborrheica
   d) herpes
   ____

87. Patches of dry, white scales on the scalp or skin may indicate the presence of:
   a) psoriasis
   b) eczema
   c) venenata
   d) naevus
   ____

88. Herpes simplex, or fever blisters, usually occur around the:
   a) scalp
   b) ears
   c) eyes
   d) lips
   ____

89. A chronic inflammatory congestion of the cheeks and nose characterized by redness and dilation of the blood vessels is called:
   a) milia
   b) asteatosis
   c) seborrhea
   d) rosacea
   ____

90. Eczema is a skin inflammation:
   a) of known origin
   b) of unknown origin
   c) with no lesions
   d) with no sensations
   ____

91. The technical name for fever blisters, which commonly appear on the lips, is:
   a) eczema
   b) herpes simplex
   c) rosacea
   d) pityriasis simples
   ____

92. Liver spots are known as:
    a) naevi
    b) leucoderma
    c) chloasma
    d) albinism

    ———

93. A birthmark is known as:
    a) albinism
    b) naevus
    c) leucoderma
    d) chloasma

    ———

94. Abnormal white patches on the skin are called:
    a) chloasma
    b) albinism
    c) leucoderma
    d) naevi

    ———

95. The common term for lentigines is:
    a) birthmarks
    b) freckles
    c) warts
    d) calluses

    ———

96. Continued friction of the hands and feet may result in the formation of a:
    a) naevus
    b) keloid
    c) keratoma
    d) verruca

    ———

97. A skin wart is known as a:
    a) keloid
    b) keratoma
    c) verruca
    d) naevus

    ———

98. Keratoma is the technical term for a:
    a) callus
    b) wart
    c) tumor
    d) birthmark

    ———

Removing Unwanted Hair

1. The method used for permanent hair removal is:
   a) tweezing   c) depilatory
   b) arching   d) electrology   ____

2. An excessive growth of hair is called:
   a) papilla   c) hypertrichosis
   b) thermolysis   d) trichoptilosis   ____

3. The known causes of superfluous hair are hormonal imbalances, drugs, and:
   a) heredity   c) alopecia
   b) contagion   d) senility   ____

4. Electrology may be given by the galvanic method or the:
   a) electrode method   c) positive pole method
   b) shortwave method   d) depilation method   ____

5. The shortwave method of electrolysis uses:
   a) a triple needle   c) a double needle
   b) a single needle   d) multiple needles   ____

6. The multiple needle method of electrolysis is known as the:
   a) shortwave method   c) coagulation method
   b) electrode method   d) galvanic method   ____

7. The galvanic method decomposes the hair:
   a) papilla   c) keratin
   b) follicle   d) medulla   ____

8. One area that should *never* have an electrolysis treatment is the:
   a) chin   c) upper arm
   b) inner nose   d) legs   ____

9. The necessity for the electrologist to keep close watch on the time is eliminated by:
   a) intensity controls   c) deep insertion
   b) receptacle controls   d) automatic timing   ____

10. When the need arises for more current, increase the:
    a) timing   c) intensity
    b) insertion   d) fluorescence   ____

11. Hair may be temporarily removed by:
    a) diathermy   c) shortwaves
    b) depilatories   d) galvanic current   ____

12. Hair usually is removed from the armpits by:
    a) diathermy   c) hot wax
    b) depilatories   d) shaving   ____

13. Superfluous hair usually is removed from the eyebrows and chin by:
    a) shaving
    b) diothergy
    c) tweezing
    d) a and b
    ___

14. Cream, paste, or powder hair removers are called chemical:
    a) emollients
    b) electrolysis
    c) diathermy
    d) depilatories
    ___

15. After the removal of a wax depilatory, apply an emollient cream or a/an:
    a) disinfectant
    b) deodorant
    c) caustic
    d) antiseptic
    ___

16. Before applying a chemical depilatory, it is necessary to give a:
    a) hair test
    b) strand test
    c) skin test
    d) acid test
    ___

17. Cold wax is removed from the treatment area with:
    a) tweezers
    b) solvent
    c) cotton cloth
    d) gloves
    ___

18. For those clients who cannot tolerate hot wax, another method available for the temporary removal of superfluous hair is:
    a) cold wax
    b) electrolysis
    c) thermolysis
    d) diathermy
    ___

19. A wax type of depilatory usually is recommended for the upper lip, cheeks, and:
    a) chin
    b) ears
    c) hands
    d) elbows
    ___

20. Wax must never be applied over warts, moles, growths, or abrasions because it may cause a/an:
    a) allergy
    b) discoloration
    c) irritation
    d) carbuncle
    ___

21. It is necessary to test the heated wax before applying it to the skin to prevent skin:
    a) infection
    b) contagion
    c) coagulation
    d) burns
    ___

Cells, Anatomy, and Physiology

1. Cells are the basic units of:
   a) dead matter
   b) living matter
   c) chemicals
   d) cosmetics
   _____

2. Protoplasm, a colorless jellylike substance, is found in:
   a) all cells
   b) disinfectants
   c) facial creams
   d) chemical solutions
   _____

3. Food materials for cellular growth and self-repair are found in the:
   a) nucleus
   b) membrane
   c) cytoplasm
   d) centrosome
   _____

4. The nucleus of the cell controls its:
   a) growth
   b) self-repair
   c) secretions
   d) reproduction
   _____

5. When cells need to be replaced, they:
   a) stop growing
   b) reproduce
   c) gradually die
   d) dry up
   _____

6. Metabolism consists of two phases—anabolism and:
   a) mitosis
   b) excretion
   c) amitosis
   d) catabolism
   _____

7. Body cells grow and reproduce during:
   a) anabolism
   b) catabolism
   c) mitosis
   d) amitosis
   _____

8. The energy needed for muscular effort is released during:
   a) mitosis
   b) amitosis
   c) anabolism
   d) catabolism
   _____

9. Tissue is a group of similar:
   a) bacteria
   b) plants
   c) minerals
   d) cells
   _____

10. The heart, lungs, liver, kidneys, stomach, and intestines are body _____.
    a) systems
    b) tissues
    c) organs
    d) secretions
    _____

11. Groups of organs that carry out a life activity of the body are called:
    a) tissues
    b) systems
    c) colonies
    d) glands
    _____

12. How many systems are there in the body?
    a) 1
    b) 3
    c) 10
    d) 15
    _____

13. The skeletal system is important because it:
    a) covers and shapes the body
    b) supplies the body with blood
    c) is the physical foundation of the body
    d) carries nerve messages
    _____

14. The hardest structure of the body is:
    a) muscle
    b) nerve
    c) bone
    d) ligament
    _____

15. One of the functions of bones is to:
    a) stimulate the blood circulation
    b) expand muscles
    c) give shape and support to the body
    d) contract muscles
    _____

16. The scientific study of the bones, their structure and functions, is called:
    a) myology
    b) technology
    c) osteology
    d) biology
    _____

17. The functions of the skull are to shape the head and protect the:
    a) periosteum
    b) brain
    c) ligaments
    d) sphenoid
    _____

18. An important function of bones is to:
    a) stimulate blood circulation
    b) protect the organs
    c) stimulate the muscles
    d) create calcium
    _____

19. Bone consists of about two-thirds mineral matter and one-third:
    a) animal matter
    b) liquid matter
    c) gaseous matter
    d) chemical matter
    _____

20. The cranial bones that are not affected by massage are the sphenoid and the:
    a) occipital
    b) ethmoid
    c) temporal
    d) frontal
    _____

21. The small fragile bones located at the front part of the inner wall of the eye sockets are the:
    a) nasal bones
    b) zygomatic bones
    c) lacrimal bones
    d) maxillae bones
    _____

22. The largest and strongest bone of the face is the:
    a) lacrimal
    b) maxillae
    c) mandible
    d) zygomatic
    _____

23. The place of union or junction of two or more bones is called a:
    a) ligament
    b) cartilage
    c) synovia
    d) joint
    _____

24. The skull consists of eight cranial bones and:
    a) 8 facial bones
    b) 10 facial bones
    c) 12 facial bones
    d) 14 facial bones
    _____

25. The skull is the:
    a) bone of the arm
    b) skeleton of the head
    c) facial nerve of the head
    d) bone of the neck   ____

26. The occipital bone forms the back and base of the:
    a) neck
    b) cranium
    c) upper jaw
    d) forehead   ____

27. The parietal bones form the top and sides of the:
    a) face
    b) cranium
    c) cheeks
    d) neck   ____

28. The frontal bone forms the:
    a) upper jaw
    b) lower jaw
    c) forehead
    d) cheek   ____

29. The temporal bones form the:
    a) forehead
    b) lower jaw
    c) Adam's apple
    d) sides of the head   ____

30. The ethmoid bone is situated:
    a) at the temple
    b) at the side of the cranium
    c) between the eye sockets
    d) on top of the cranium   ____

31. The nasal bones form the:
    a) tip of the nose
    b) back of the nose
    c) bridge of the nose
    d) inner walls of the nose   ____

32. The zygomatic, or malar, bones form the:
    a) outer walls of the nose
    b) mouth
    c) cheeks
    d) "U" shaped bone in
       the throat   ____

33. Maxillae are bones that form the:
    a) lower jaw
    b) upper jaw
    c) eye socket
    d) forehead   ____

34. The mandible bone forms the:
    a) upper jaw
    b) lower jaw
    c) cheek
    d) nose   ____

35. The cervical vertebrae form the upper part of the spinal column
    in the:
    a) neck region
    b) front of the neck
    c) side of the neck
    d) front of the skull   ____

36. The sphenoid bone joins together all bones of the:
    a) nose
    b) cranium
    c) ear
    d) neck   ____

37. One of the functions of the muscular system is to:
    a) circulate the blood
    b) nourish the body
    c) produce body
       movements
    d) produce marrow   ____

38. Muscles consist of:
    a) continuous sheets of cords or sinews
    b) elastic bundles of tissue
    c) contractile fibrous tissue
    d) nonelastic bundles of tissue ____

39. The more fixed attachment of a muscle is called:
    a) origin of muscle
    b) insertion of muscle
    c) muscle tone
    d) ligament ____

40. The more movable attachment of a muscle is called:
    a) insertion of muscle
    b) origin of muscle
    c) body of muscle
    d) aponeurosis ____

41. The part of the muscle between the origin and the insertion is the:
    a) tendon
    b) belly
    c) fascia
    d) aponeurosis ____

42. Muscles controlled by the will are called:
    a) involuntary muscles
    b) voluntary muscles
    c) cardiac muscles
    d) nonstriated muscles ____

43. Muscles not controlled by the will are called:
    a) skeletal muscles
    b) voluntary muscles
    c) involuntary muscles
    d) striated muscles ____

44. The cardiac muscle is found in the:
    a) stomach
    b) heart
    c) lungs
    d) intestines ____

45. The study of the structure, functions, and diseases of the muscles is called:
    a) striation
    b) mentalis
    c) myology
    d) osteology ____

46. In massage, pressure is usually directed on the muscles from the:
    a) insertion to the origin
    b) origin to the insertion
    c) belly to the insertion
    d) fixed attachment to the movable ____

47. For its activities, the muscular system is dependent upon the skeletal system and the:
    a) lymphatic system
    b) digestive system
    c) nervous system
    d) circulatory system ____

48. The muscles cover, shape, and support the:
    a) skeletal system
    b) nervous system
    c) circulatory system
    d) digestive system ____

49. The epicranius muscle covers the:
    a) side of head
    b) top of skull
    c) bottom of skull
    d) cheekbone ____

50. The orbicularis oculi is a muscle that surrounds the margin of the:
    a) mouth
    b) nose
    c) eye socket
    d) head
    ____

51. The corrugator extends along the:
    a) side of nose
    b) eyebrow line
    c) front of ear
    d) side of cheek
    ____

52. The procerus is a muscle of the:
    a) eye
    b) nose
    c) ear
    d) mouth
    ____

53. The front and back parts of the epicranius muscle are connected by a:
    a) procerus
    b) tendon
    c) frontalis
    d) mentalis
    ____

54. The quadratus labii superioris is the muscle that raises the:
    a) ear
    b) eye
    c) upper lip
    d) lower lip
    ____

55. The quadratus labii inferioris is the muscle that draws back the:
    a) upper lip
    b) lower lip
    c) eyebrow
    d) eyelid
    ____

56. The orbicularis oris is the muscle that closes the:
    a) eyes
    b) lips
    c) nostrils
    d) ears
    ____

57. The mentalis is a muscle located in the:
    a) upper lip
    b) eyelid
    c) jaw
    d) chin
    ____

58. The muscle that rotates the shoulder blades and controls the swinging movement of the arm is the:
    a) risorius
    b) masseter
    c) trapezius
    d) platysma
    ____

59. The sternocleidomastoid muscle:
    a) dilates the nostrils
    b) closes the lips
    c) closes the eyes
    d) rotates the head
    ____

60. The epicranius consists of two parts, the frontalis and the:
    a) corrugator
    b) caninus
    c) risorius
    d) occipitalis
    ____

61. The nervous system controls and coordinates all body:
    a) structures
    b) functions
    c) diseases
    d) cleanliness
    ____

62. The nervous system is composed of the brain and spinal cord and their:
    a) blood vessels
    b) nerves
    c) lymphatics
    d) glands
    ____

63. A neuron is a structural unit of the:
    a) skeletal system   c) muscular system
    b) nervous system   d) circulatory system   _____

64. Nerves are long, white cords made up of fibers from the:
    a) nerve cells   c) bone cells
    b) muscle cells   d) blood cells   _____

65. The sensory nerves carry messages from the:
    a) brain to the muscles   c) brain to the spinal cord
    b) sense organs to the brain d) brain to the bones   _____

66. The motor nerves carry nerve impulses from the:
    a) sense organs to the brain c) muscles to the brain
    b) brain to the muscles   d) skin to the brain   _____

67. The main divisions of the nervous system are the autonomic
    system, peripheral system, and the:
    a) lymphatic system   c) spinal cord
    b) ganglia system   d) cerebrospinal system   _____

68. The cerebrospinal nervous system controls the:
    a) stomach muscles   c) involuntary muscles
    b) heart muscles   d) voluntary muscles   _____

69. Nerves going to all parts of the body originate in the brain and
    the:
    a) sense organs   c) spinal cord
    b) muscles   d) heart   _____

70. Twelve pairs of cranial nerves branch out from the brain and
    reach various parts of the:
    a) arms and hands   c) abdomen and back
    b) legs and feet   d) head, face, and neck   _____

71. Thirty-one pairs of nerves extend from the:
    a) brain   c) head
    b) spinal cord   d) face   _____

72. The two divisions of the autonomic nervous system are the
    sympathetic and _____ systems.
    a) parasympathetic   c) central nervous
    b) peripheral   d) apathetic   _____

73. An automatic response to a stimulus is called:
    a) mental nerve   c) radial nerve
    b) reflex   d) repetition   _____

74. Which of the following is NOT one of the three branches of the
    fifth cranial, or trifacial, nerve?
    a) mandibular   c) ophthalmic
    b) greater occipital   d) maxillary   _____

75. Which nerve affects the muscles of the neck and back?
The _____ cranial nerve.
   a) fifth
   b) seventh
   c) eleventh
   d) thirteenth _____

76. The trifacial is the chief sensory nerve of the:
   a) arm
   b) face
   c) chest
   d) shoulder _____

77. The skin of the forehead and eyebrows is supplied by the:
   a) supraorbital nerve
   b) infraorbital nerve
   c) supratrochlear nerve
   d) infratrochlear nerve _____

78. The skin of the lower lip and chin is supplied by the:
   a) infraorbital nerve
   b) supraorbital nerve
   c) mental nerve
   d) optic nerve _____

79. The skin of the upper lip and side of nose is supplied by the:
   a) infraorbital nerve
   b) supraorbital nerve
   c) optic nerve
   d) auricular nerve _____

80. The seventh cranial nerve is also known as the:
   a) facial nerve
   b) trifacial nerve
   c) trigeminal nerve
   d) cervical nerve _____

81. The seventh cranial nerve is the chief motor nerve of the:
   a) arm
   b) chest
   c) face
   d) shoulder _____

82. The zygomatic motor nerve affects the muscles of the upper part of the:
   a) mouth
   b) cheek
   c) chin
   d) nose _____

83. The temporal nerve affects the muscles of the forehead, temple, and:
   a) nose
   b) upper lip
   c) lower lip
   d) eyebrow _____

84. Most of the muscles of the mouth are supplied by the:
   a) cervical nerve
   b) accessory nerve
   c) buccal nerve
   d) temporal nerve _____

85. The blood-vascular system comprises the heart, arteries, veins, and:
   a) lymph nodes
   b) lacteals
   c) duct glands
   d) capillaries _____

86. The heart is a cone-shaped organ located in the:
   a) chest cavity
   b) abdominal cavity
   c) stomach
   d) ducts _____

87. The back flow of blood in the veins is prevented by:
   a) valves
   b) vessels
   c) vesicles
   d) vehicles _____

88. The upper heart chambers are called:
   a) ventricles
   b) atria
   c) valves
   d) pericardia
   _____

89. The lower heart chambers are called:
   a) ventricles
   b) arteries
   c) valves
   d) atria
   _____

90. Vessels that carry blood away from the heart are called:
   a) veins
   b) arteries
   c) capillaries
   d) lymphatics
   _____

91. Vessels that carry blood to the heart are called:
   a) veins
   b) capillaries
   c) arteries
   d) lacteals
   _____

92. Body cells receive food and eliminate waste products through the walls of:
   a) veins
   b) arteries
   c) capillaries
   d) lacteals
   _____

93. The fluid part of the blood is called:
   a) plasma
   b) white blood cells
   c) red blood cells
   d) thrombocytes
   _____

94. Blood cells carrying oxygen to the cells are called:
   a) white corpuscles
   b) blood platelets
   c) red corpuscles
   d) hemoglobin
   _____

95. Blood cells that fight harmful bacteria are called:
   a) platelets
   b) white corpuscles
   c) red corpuscles
   d) thrombocytes
   _____

96. Those parts of the body not reached by the blood are nourished by:
   a) sweat
   b) sebum
   c) juices
   d) lymph
   _____

97. The common carotid artery is located at the side of the:
   a) head
   b) face
   c) neck
   d) nose
   _____

98. Blood reaches the outer parts of the head, face, and neck by way of the:
   a) internal carotid artery
   b) internal jugular vein
   c) external carotid artery
   d) external jugular vein
   _____

99. The lower region of the face is supplied by the:
   a) occipital artery
   b) external maxillary artery
   c) posterior artery
   d) frontal artery
   _____

100. The parietal artery supplies the:
   a) forehead
   b) back of head
   c) crown and side of head
   d) cheeks
   _____

101. The frontal artery supplies the:
    a) back of head   c) forehead
    b) crown   d) side of nose   _____

102. The supraorbital artery supplies the:
    a) lip   c) forehead
    b) nose   d) ear   _____

103. The inferior labial artery supplies the:
    a) lower lip   c) nose
    b) upper lip   d) eyebrow   _____

104. The submental artery supplies the:
    a) chin   c) nose
    b) upper lip   d) ear   _____

105. The superior labial artery supplies the:
    a) chin   c) upper lip
    b) lower lip   d) back of ear   _____

106. Blood is supplied to the brain, eye sockets, eyelids, and forehead by the:
    a) labial artery   c) jugular artery
    b) internal carotid artery   d) orbital artery   _____

107. The external jugular vein returns the blood to the heart from the:
    a) brain   c) head, face, and neck
    b) shoulders   d) chest   _____

108. The occipital artery supplies blood to the region of the:
    a) back of head   c) front of head
    b) mouth and nose   d) cheeks   _____

109. The palm of the hand contains:
    a) 8 carpal bones   c) 10 phalanges
    b) 5 metacarpal bones   d) 6 dorsal bones   _____

110. The ulna is a large bone of the:
    a) wrist   c) upper arm
    b) hand   d) forearm   _____

111. The wrist bones are called the:
    a) carpal bones   c) digital bones
    b) metacarpal bones   d) radial bones   _____

112. The longest and largest bone of the arm is the:
    a) ulna   c) humerus
    b) radius   d) clavicle   _____

113. The function of the extensor muscles is to:
    a) straighten the hands and fingers   c) close the hands and fingers
    b) rotate the wrist   d) separate the fingers   _____

114. The function of the flexor muscles is to:
    a) open the hands and fingers
    b) bend the wrists and fingers
    c) rotate the hands and fingers
    d) adduct the fingers
    ___

115. The fingers of the hand are separated by movement of the:
    a) abductor muscles
    b) pronator muscles
    c) flexor muscles
    d) extensor muscles
    ___

116. The ulnar nerve supplies the:
    a) thumb side of the arm
    b) little finger side of the arm
    c) back of the hand
    d) top side of the fingers
    ___

117. The radial nerve supplies the:
    a) little finger side of the arm
    b) palm of the hand
    c) thumb side of the arm
    d) index finger
    ___

118. The flexor muscles are necessary for:
    a) bending the wrists
    b) straightening the wrists
    c) rotating the fingers
    d) straightening the fingers
    ___

119. The digital nerves supply the:
    a) upper arm
    b) forearm
    c) back of the wrist
    d) fingers
    ___

Electricity and Light Therapy

1. Magnetic, chemical, and heat effects are produced by:
   a) an open circuit
   b) a short circuit
   c) a broken circuit
   d) electricity   ____

2. A substance that readily transmits an electric current is a/an:
   a) conductor
   b) nonconductor
   c) insulator
   d) converter   ____

3. A substance that resists the passage of an electric current is a/an:
   a) insulator
   b) conductor
   c) converter
   d) rectifier   ____

4. Rubber and silk are:
   a) conductors
   b) insulators
   c) electrodes
   d) converters   ____

5. A metal, such as copper wire, is a/an:
   a) nonconductor of electricity
   b) conductor of electricity
   c) insulator of electricity
   d) converter of electricity   ____

6. In electricity, electrodes serve the same purpose as:
   a) converters of electricity
   b) insulators of electricity
   c) nonconductors of electricity
   d) conductors of electricity   ____

7. A constant electrical current flowing in one direction is called a/an:
   a) alternating current
   b) direct current
   c) faradic current
   d) AC current   ____

8. An electrical current flowing first in one direction and then in the opposite direction is called a/an:
   a) direct current
   b) Tesla current
   c) alternating current
   d) galvanic current   ____

9. A constant and direct current used to produce chemical effects on the tissues and fluids of the body is the:
   a) faradic current
   b) sinusoidal current
   c) Tesla current
   d) galvanic current   ____

10. An alternating and interrupted current, used principally to cause muscular contractions, is the:
    a) faradic current
    b) high-frequency current
    c) Tesla current
    d) galvanic current   ____

11. A unit of electrical pressure is referred to as a/an:
    a) ampere
    b) volt
    c) ohm
    d) watt   ____

12. An ampere is a unit of electrical:
    a) pressure
    b) resistance
    c) tension
    d) strength   ____

13. An ohm is a unit of electrical:
   a) strength
   b) pressure
   c) resistance
   d) tension
   ____

14. A 1/1000 part of an ampere is called a:
   a) voltmeter
   b) kilowatt
   c) watt
   d) milliampere
   ____

15. A milliamperemeter measures the rate of flow of:
   a) water
   b) an electric current
   c) light
   d) heat
   ____

16. The high-frequency current commonly used in the beauty salon is the:
   a) d'Arsonval current
   b) Oudin current
   c) Tesla current
   d) sinusoidal current
   ____

17. The Tesla current is commonly called the:
   a) ultraviolet ray
   b) violet ray
   c) low-frequency current
   d) infrared ray
   ____

18. An electrical current used for its heat-producing effects is the:
   a) galvanic current
   b) faradic current
   c) high-frequency current
   d) sinusoidal current
   ____

19. A glass electrode that gives off sparks operates on:
   a) galvanic current
   b) faradic current
   c) sinusoidal current
   d) high-frequency current
   ____

20. For a stimulating effect, the high-frequency electrode is:
   a) slightly lifted from the skin by the cosmetologist
   b) held by the client
   c) kept in close contact with the skin
   d) turned very low
   ____

21. The vibrator is an electrical appliance that:
   a) reduces blood circulation
   b) weakens the area being treated
   c) stimulates the area being treated
   d) lightens the area being treated
   ____

22. Facial and scalp steamers are used in the salon to supply:
   a) dry heat at a constant temperature
   b) moist heat at a constant temperature
   c) dry heat at an uneven temperature
   d) moist heat at an uneven temperature
   ____

23. Treatment by means of light rays is called light:
   a) therapy
   b) density
   c) energy
   d) tinea
   ____

24. About 80% of natural sunshine consists of:
   a) ultraviolet rays
   b) actinic rays
   c) visible light rays
   d) infrared rays
   ____

25. The shortest and least penetrating light rays of the spectrum are the:
   a) infrared rays
   b) ultraviolet rays
   c) orange light rays
   d) red light rays
   ____

26. The light rays of the spectrum that are pure heat rays are:
   a) ultraviolet rays
   b) actinic rays
   c) blue light rays
   d) infrared rays
   ____

27. Before applying light rays, use cotton pads saturated in a witch hazel or boric acid solution to protect the client's:
   a) ears
   b) nose
   c) eyes
   d) mouth
   ____

28. Resistance to disease may be increased by:
   a) red rays
   b) infrared rays
   c) white light rays
   d) ultraviolet rays
   ____

29. The skin can tan if it is exposed to:
   a) white dermal light
   b) red dermal light
   c) infrared rays
   d) ultraviolet rays
   ____

30. The shorter rays reach the skin when the ultraviolet ray lamp is placed within:
   a) 36" from the body
   b) 12" from the body
   c) 30" from the body
   d) 40" from the body
   ____

31. Both the cosmetologist and client must wear safety eye wear to protect their eyes when exposed to:
   a) violet rays
   b) ultraviolet rays
   c) white dermal light
   d) red dermal light
   ____

32. Before using an ultraviolet lamp, the skin should:
   a) be coated with olive oil
   b) be thoroughly cleansed
   c) be bare
   d) not be cleansed
   ____

33. Deep heating of body tissues is the main effect of:
   a) blue light
   b) violet light
   c) ultraviolet rays
   d) infrared rays
   ____

34. The average distance to place an infrared lamp from the skin is about:
   a) 5"
   b) 10"
   c) 18"
   d) 30"
   ____

Chemistry

1. Organic chemistry is the study of all substances containing:
   a) carbon
   b) hydrogen
   c) lead
   d) water
   _____

2. The branch of chemistry that deals with products containing carbon is called:
   a) atomic chemistry
   b) organic chemistry
   c) inorganic chemistry
   d) molecular chemistry
   _____

3. Matter is anything that:
   a) floats on water
   b) is water resistant
   c) reacts to carbon
   d) occupies space
   _____

4. Desks, chairs, wood, and walls have a definite form, and therefore are examples of:
   a) solids
   b) elements
   c) gases
   d) bases
   _____

5. The smallest particle of an element is the:
   a) atom
   b) base
   c) proton
   d) electron
   _____

6. The simplest form of matter that cannot be decomposed by chemical means is a/an:
   a) element
   b) compound
   c) synthesis
   d) emulsion
   _____

7. Substances that cannot be reduced to simpler substances are:
   a) bases
   b) solutes
   c) elements
   d) gases
   _____

8. Iron, sulfur, oxygen, zinc, and silver are all examples of:
   a) compounds
   b) mixtures
   c) molecules
   d) elements
   _____

9. The formation of a new product by the uniting of two or more elements is known as a:
   a) compound
   b) analysis
   c) synthetic
   d) hormone
   _____

10. When two or more elements combine chemically, they form a new substance called a:
    a) mixture
    b) compound
    c) suspension
    d) solution
    _____

11. A product that contains both hydrogen and oxygen and turns red litmus paper blue is a/an:
    a) salt
    b) acid
    c) base
    d) solid
    _____

12. When the hydrogen in an acid is replaced by a metal, the result is a/an:
   a) alkali
   b) alcohol
   c) salt
   d) oxide
   ____

13. Sodium chloride is an example of:
   a) soft water
   b) distilled water
   c) a salt
   d) a soap
   ____

14. A combination of substances that are held together by physical rather than chemical ties is called a:
   a) mixture
   b) compound
   c) synthesis
   d) solvent
   ____

15. An alteration of the properties of a substance without the formation of any new substance is a:
   a) mixture
   b) chemical change
   c) compound
   d) physical change
   ____

16. The most abundant element is:
   a) oxygen
   b) hydrogen
   c) nitrogen
   d) ammonia
   ____

17. The second most abundant element known is:
   a) peroxide
   b) oxygen
   c) nitrogen
   d) hydrogen
   ____

18. Pure water with a pH of 7 is considered to be:
   a) neutral
   b) acid
   c) alkaline
   d) salty
   ____

19. A soap solution with a pH factor of 10 would be considered to be a/an:
   a) acid
   b) salt
   c) alkali
   d) oxide
   ____

20. Water is composed of:
   a) 2 volumes of hydrogen and 1 volume of oxygen
   b) 2 volumes of hydrogen and 2 volumes of oxygen
   c) 1 volume of hydrogen and 2 volumes of oxygen
   d) 1 volume of hydrogen and 1 volume of oxygen
   ____

21. Removing impurities from water by passing it through a porous substance is the process of:
   a) distillation
   b) neutralization
   c) filtration
   d) oxidation
   ____

22. What type of change occurs when ice melts and becomes water? A _____ change.
   a) chemical
   b) physical
   c) specific gravity
   d) mixture
   ____

23. The ability of a substance to resist scratching refers to its:
   a) color
   b) hardness
   c) acidity
   d) specific gravity
   ____

24. Lighting a match or burning wood is an example of:
    a) slow oxidation
    b) neutralization
    c) retardation
    d) rapid oxidation ____

25. If a product has a pH of 9.5, it is a/an:
    a) neutral
    b) balanced item
    c) acid
    d) alkaline ____

26. The pH of hair is:
    a) 2.5–3.5
    b) 3.5–4.5
    c) 4.5–5.5
    d) 7.0–8.5 ____

27. Shampoos that lather freely in both hard and soft water are:
    a) glycerine shampoos
    b) nonstrip shampoos
    c) anionic shampoos
    d) borax shampoos ____

28. A substance used to even porosity of overporous hair before a permanent-wave lotion is applied is a/an:
    a) thio solution
    b) alkali
    c) filler
    d) neutralizer ____

29. The two types of chemical hair relaxers are the thio relaxer and:
    a) sodium hydroxide relaxer
    b) keratin relaxer
    c) ammonium relaxer
    d) polypeptide relaxer ____

30. In order to help restore natural oils to dry and damaged hair, use:
    a) a hair conditioner
    b) a soapless shampoo
    c) amino acid
    d) keratin ____

31. What does temporary haircoloring contain?
    a) protein colors
    b) developers
    c) ammonium colors
    d) certified colors ____

32. In permanent hair tinting, hydrogen peroxide is used as a:
    a) conditioner
    b) developer
    c) filler
    d) relaxer ____

33. Chemical agents designed to remove artificial color from the hair are:
    a) relaxers
    b) dye solvents
    c) developers
    d) fillers ____

34. A preparation made by dissolving a solid, liquid, or gaseous substance in another substance is a/an:
    a) suspension
    b) ointment
    c) solution
    d) powder ____

35. In the creation of a solution, the liquid used to dissolve a substance is called the:
    a) solute
    b) suspension
    c) solvent
    d) emulsion ____

36. Solvents that mix easily are:
    a) immiscible
    b) miscible
    c) incompatible
    d) volatile ____

37. A permanent mixture of two or more substances that are united with the aid of a binder (gum) is a/an:
   a) ointment
   b) emulsion
   c) suspension
   d) solution
   _____

38. A semisolid mixture of an organic substance and a medicinal agent is a/an:
   a) soap
   b) zinc oxide
   c) ointment
   d) sulfonated oil
   _____

39. Soap is formed from the chemical combination of:
   a) an alkali and fat or oil
   b) an alkali and a salt
   c) a detergent and potassium
   d) a fat and alcohol
   _____

40. Witch hazel is a solution that works as:
   a) an astringent
   b) zinc oxide
   c) hormones
   d) boric acid
   _____

41. Good soaps should contain a minimum of:
   a) animal fats
   b) vegetable oils
   c) free alkali
   d) glycerine and oil
   _____

42. Temporary mixtures of two kinds of matter are:
   a) solutions
   b) emulsions
   c) suspensions
   d) mixtures
   _____

43. An agent that neutralizes or destroys disagreeable odor is a/an:
   a) emollient
   b) hormone
   c) astringent
   d) deodorant
   _____

44. The basic purpose of a cold cream is to:
   a) eradicate wrinkles
   b) cleanse skin
   c) strengthen facial muscles
   d) reduce fat cells
   _____

45. An alkaline causes the hair to:
   a) harden and shrink
   b) soften and swell
   c) decrease in porosity
   d) increase in density
   _____

46. If a product has a pH of 2.0, it is a/an:
   a) neutral
   b) balanced item
   c) acid
   d) alkaline
   _____

47. A cream used for lubricating the skin during massage is a/an:
   a) hormone cream
   b) vanishing cream
   c) massage cream
   d) cleansing cream
   _____

48. A good face powder should contain:
   a) talcum
   b) pure white lead
   c) alum powder
   d) starch
   _____

49. A cream is recommended for skin that is:
   a) scaly
   b) oily
   c) dry
   d) parched
   _____

The Salon Business

1. When planning to open a beauty salon, careful consideration must be given to the selection of:
   a) depreciation
   b) student enrollment
   c) a location
   d) a mortgage
   ____

2. A good location for a beauty salon is near a:
   a) supermarket
   b) machine shop
   c) bowling alley
   d) tavern
   ____

3. A salon owner should protect against unexpected increases in rent by negotiating a/an:
   a) insurance policy
   b) mortgage
   c) compensation certificate
   d) lease
   ____

4. Building maintenance and renovations are regulated by:
   a) federal laws
   b) local ordinances
   c) state laws
   d) interstate regulations
   ____

5. State laws usually cover sales tax, licensure, and:
   a) excise taxes
   b) worker's compensation
   c) Social Security
   d) pure drug regulations
   ____

6. In addition to income tax and cosmetic and luxury taxes, federal laws cover:
   a) Social Security
   b) building codes
   c) sales taxes
   d) licensing
   ____

7. Salon owners purchase insurance policies to protect themselves against suits for:
   a) malingering
   b) overcharging
   c) malpractice
   d) licensure
   ____

8. Careful planning of the salon is essential in order to achieve economy and maximum:
   a) parking
   b) public transportation
   c) rental
   d) efficiency
   ____

9. In a well-organized beauty salon, the flow of clients is directed toward the:
   a) reception area
   b) shampooing area
   c) dispensary
   d) powder room
   ____

10. One of the best promotional aids available to the salon owner is an attractive, comfortable:
    a) dispensary
    b) salon office
    c) reception area
    d) shampoo area
    ____

11. For satisfactory service, it is essential that the salon have within it good plumbing and sufficient:
    a) office space
    b) lighting
    c) parking facilities
    d) transportation
    ____

12. The best form of advertising is a:
    a) neon sign
    b) pleased client
    c) newspaper ad
    d) window pane ___

13. All activities that attract attention to the salon are included under the general heading of:
    a) public service
    b) business regulation
    c) advertising
    d) planning ___

14. More intimate contact with prospective clients is created by:
    a) newspaper advertising
    b) radio advertising
    c) television advertising
    d) direct mail advertising ___

15. Salons can be located near each other if each of them:
    a) has a different type of clientele
    b) has the same type of clientele
    c) practices unethical behavior
    d) is very similar to the other one ___

16. Social Security is covered under _____ laws.
    a) local
    b) state
    c) federal
    d) income tax ___

17. Smooth salon operations are usually the result of:
    a) efficient management
    b) insufficient capital
    c) business neglect
    d) careless controls ___

18. The largest expense item in operating a beauty salon is:
    a) rent
    b) salaries
    c) supplies
    d) advertising ___

19. The largest items of beauty salon expense are salaries, rent, advertising, and:
    a) supplies
    b) laundry
    c) lighting
    d) telephone ___

20. Beauty salon services are considered in the appointment book in terms of:
    a) difficulty
    b) color
    c) time
    d) style ___

21. Salon and individual licenses are covered by _____ laws.
    a) federal
    b) income tax
    c) local
    d) state ___

22. An important part of the beauty salon's business is performed by:
    a) mail
    b) telephone
    c) messenger
    d) business meetings ___

23. Good telephone habits and techniques help to build up the salon's:
    a) reputation
    b) appearance
    c) location
    d) gossip ___

24. The most important use of the telephone in the salon is to:
    a) make appointments
    b) keep up with local gossip
    c) make personal dates
    d) keep employees happy ____

25. Salon business can be promoted effectively over the telephone, provided there is:
    a) time to waste
    b) business neglect
    c) good planning
    d) sufficient capital ____

26. Assigning a well-trained person to handle telephone calls is evidence of:
    a) wasted talent
    b) poor management
    c) business inexperience
    d) good planning ____

27. A very important area of good planning is to have the telephone in the proper:
    a) color
    b) location
    c) style
    d) texture ____

28. Building requirements and renovations are covered by _____ laws.
    a) local
    b) state
    c) income tax
    d) federal ____

29. A good salon telephone technique requires that the receptionist at all times be:
    a) defensive
    b) tactful
    c) apologetic
    d) abrupt ____

30. When calling a beauty salon, clients appreciate receptionists who are:
    a) abrupt
    b) indifferent
    c) impatient
    d) courteous ____

31. A clear speaking voice, correct speech, and a pleasant tone are requisites of a good telephone:
    a) personality
    b) posture
    c) transformation
    d) instrument ____

32. To create a good impression over the phone:
    a) speak very rapidly
    b) use correct grammar
    c) use a hesitant manner
    d) speak very slowly ____

33. For proper telephone conversation, your pronunciation should be:
    a) garbled
    b) musical
    c) slurred
    d) precise ____

34. A very important responsibility in the salon operation is the handling of salon:
    a) messengers
    b) socials
    c) appointments
    d) personal calls ____

35. Proper spacing of appointments permits the salon to operate:
   a) efficiently
   b) inconveniently
   c) irresponsibly
   d) socially
   ___

36. An especially difficult but important telephone duty is:
   a) adjusting complaints
   b) making social calls
   c) answering personal calls
   d) discouraging clients
   ___

37. When adjusting complaints over the phone, it is important to use tact, courtesy, and:
   a) arrogance
   b) self-control
   c) interruptions
   d) impatience
   ___

38. When listening to a client's complaint, it is important to avoid:
   a) being sympathetic
   b) promising free service
   c) interrupting them
   d) apologizing
   ___

39. The properly used telephone is an important and valuable aid in:
   a) increasing business
   b) reducing service
   c) avoiding creditors
   d) disparaging your competitor
   ___

40. In order to make selling agreeable and productive, the cosmetologist must be:
   a) self-confident
   b) impatient
   c) overbearing
   d) ingratiating
   ___

41. The first step in successful selling in the beauty salon is to:
   a) break down resistance
   b) discourage competition
   c) sell yourself
   d) be aggressive
   ___

42. The personal factor that contributes most to bringing clients back to the salon is the cosmetologist's:
   a) aggressiveness
   b) familiarity
   c) gossip
   d) personality
   ___

43. A salon that is owned by stockholders and that has a state charter is known as a/an:
   a) corporation
   b) individual ownership
   c) partnership
   d) joint ownership
   ___

44. Before people will buy beauty services or products, they must be:
   a) discouraged
   b) motivated
   c) pressured
   d) deceived
   ___

45. The foundation of good salesmanship is:
   a) sincerity
   b) aggressiveness
   c) assertiveness
   d) determination
   ___

46. If a salon is sold, the sales agreement should contain within it all of the following EXCEPT:
   a) a written purchase agreement
   b) an inventory statement
   c) a guarantee of profits to be made
   d) the owner's identity ___

47. The type of salon ownership where one person owns the salon is:
   a) partnership
   b) individual
   c) corporation
   d) joint ___

48. What percent of a salon's money income is spent on employee salaries and commissions?
   a) 25%
   b) 30%
   c) 50%
   d) 80% ___

49. A lease is an agreement between the salon owner and the:
   a) city
   b) building owner
   c) state
   d) salon employees ___

50. In order that sales techniques be successful, the language used should be:
   a) neutral
   b) negative
   c) positive
   d) placid ___

51. The language used in presenting a beauty service should be:
   a) simple and suggestive
   b) complex and florid
   c) flaccid and pallid
   d) boisterous and loud ___

52. No matter how good a beauty service may be, it will be difficult to sell unless there is a/an:
   a) advertising campaign
   b) sales resistance
   c) need for it
   d) negative approach ___

53. To create and maintain good relationships with clients, always address them by their:
   a) nickname
   b) familiar title
   c) hair color
   d) name ___

54. It is good professional practice to maintain complete client:
   a) nickname lists
   b) shopping lists
   c) records
   d) none of the above ___

55. If two people each own 50% of one salon, their type of salon ownership is a/an:
   a) individual
   b) chain salon
   c) corporate
   d) partnership ___

56. Every satisfied client is a potential source of new:
   a) colors
   b) gossip
   c) customers
   d) styles ___

57. Products, such as shampoo, that are sold to clients are a/an
_____ type of salon product.
   a) wholesale   c) consumption
   b) retail   d) equipment   ____

58. Local, state, and federal tax laws make it mandatory that each
business maintain proper:
   a) customer relations   c) employee lounges
   b) business records   d) sales displays   ____

59. Maintaining a simple but efficient record-keeping system is a
requirement of good:
   a) customer relations   c) sales of services
   b) sales control   d) business administration   ____

60. Keeping accurate daily records permits the salon management
to evaluate:
   a) employee relations   c) customer relations
   b) business progress   d) appointments   ____

61. In order to maintain an accurate and efficient control of supplies,
it is necessary to have an organized:
   a) inventory system   c) sales force
   b) purchase order   d) depreciation record   ____

62. Business comparisons with other years are made possible by an
analysis of:
   a) daily sales slips   c) summary sheets
   b) petty cash   d) wasted supplies   ____

63. Daily sales slips, appointment books, and petty cash books
should be retained for at least:
   a) 5 years   c) 6 months
   b) 7 years   d) 3 years   ____

64. Waste of the cosmetologist's time and loss of income may be
minimized by keeping an accurate:
   a) perpetual inventory   c) weekly summary
   b) service   d) appointment book   ____

65. An accurate reflection of the activities taking place in the salon
at any given time is indicated by the:
   a) client's records   c) daily analysis
   b) appointment book   d) petty cash book   ____

66. The type of ownership that subjects the owner to the most
limited personal loss is the:
   a) corporation   c) individual proprietorship
   b) co-ownership   d) partnership   ____

67. In a partnership form of ownership, each partner assumes:
   a) limited liability   c) unlimited liability
   b) no legal responsibility   d) no liability   ____

68. Before buying or selling any beauty salon, it is advisable to consult with a:

a) stockholder   c) client

b) lawyer   d) manufacturer   ——

69. The salon owner should protect against possible casualty losses by obtaining:

a) insurance   c) life preservers

b) sanitation   d) fire extinguishers   ——

70. It is important that every cosmetologist become thoroughly familiar with cosmetology laws and:

a) medical practice laws   c) executive laws

b) sanitary codes   d) administrative laws   ——

HINTS ON HOW TO PASS YOUR STATE BOARD EXAMINATIONS

These helpful hints have been prepared for your benefit. Read them carefully, as they will assist you in passing state exams.

To present a good appearance and feel your best at the exam, use the following checklist as a reminder.

AT THE PRACTICAL EXAM

A. Personal Appearance
1. Hands and Nails:
   ☐ Hands clean and free from stains
   ☐ Nails clean and manicured
2. Hair clean and properly styled
3. Face:
   ☐ Face clean
   ☐ Proper facial makeup
4. Teeth clean and free from stains
5. Offensive Odors
   ☐ Body odor
   ☐ Breath odor

B. Clothing Appearance
1. Uniform and Regular Clothing:
   ☐ Clean and pressed
   ☐ Neat and properly fitted
   ☐ Free from odors
2. Shoes and Stockings:
   ☐ Shoes properly fit
   ☐ Shoes clean
   ☐ Stockings clean and free from runs or wrinkles

C. Personal Habits
1. Correct standing posture
2. Correct sitting posture
3. Proper walking posture without shuffling feet

HINTS FOR PRACTICAL EXAM
1. Make sure that your hands are clean.
2. Wear a uniform that is spotless and pressed without wrinkles.
3. Use only clean and sanitized implements.
4. Observe sanitary rules during practical test.
5. Keep comb and implements out of pocket.
6. Do not wear interfering jewelry.
7. Do not wear high-heeled shoes.

8. Make certain that you have all implements, materials, and supplies required.
9. Select your model carefully for quality and length of hair.

PROPER MENTAL ATTITUDE

Adopting a calm, sensible attitude will help you overcome the nervousness often associated with the taking of an exam. Remember that exams are not given to make students fail, but to do justice to all students. State exams are given in order to find out what you know and are graded fairly. If you have been studying and reviewing your textbook and notes, there is nothing to fear.

Being well rested will help you to function efficiently on the day of the test. Be sure to get sufficient sleep on the night before the exam. Try to avoid any hurry, worry, or excitement before the exam.

AT THE WRITTEN EXAMINATION

REQUIRED SUPPLIES

When taking an exam, you will need pen, pencils, eraser, watch, required implements, admission card, and other materials.

BE ON TIME

Learn in advance how to reach the location of the exam. Allow sufficient time for travel. Being on time for the exam will save you annoyance, delay, and nervous tension.

THE WRITTEN EXAM

1. Go to your assigned room. Take your seat and get comfortable.
2. Test your pen for proper functioning. Make sure that you have all your required supplies.
3. Check watch for correct time. Write down the time limits of the exam and keep it in front of you.
4. Listen carefully to the examiner's instructions and fill out all necessary forms as directed.
5. If the instructions are in printed form, read them over carefully and follow them out exactly as indicated. If anything is not clear, ask the examiner.
6. Remember, do not sign your name on the exam paper unless told to do so by the examiner. If you have been assigned a number, place it in the proper place on the exam paper and answer sheet.
7. Be ready to start when the signal is given by the examiner.
8. See how many test items are to be answered and whether any of them are optional or required.
9. Watch your time and try to answer as many test items as possible within the time limit.
10. Read each test item carefully. Answer each one consecutively and place answers in proper spaces.
11. Do not spend too much time on any individual item. If you come across a difficult one, place a small check alongside it and return to it later. If you are doubtful about any item, place a small question mark alongside it and return to it later.

12. As the exam draws to a close, allow a few minutes to answer those items that have been left blank.
13. If you finish before the time is up, review all answers, correct mistakes, and answer doubtful items.
14. When you are finished, return the exam paper and answer sheet to the examiner.

TYPICAL STATE BOARD EXAMINATIONS
TEST 1—100 MULTIPLE CHOICE QUESTIONS

DIRECTIONS: *Carefully read each statement. Choose the word or phrase that correctly completes the meaning of each statement and write the most correct corresponding letter on top of line.*

1. A dull, sallow complexion may be an indication of:
   a) controlled disease
   b) a balanced diet
   c) adequate rest
   d) poor health
   _____

2. Public hygiene also is known as:
   a) personal hygiene
   b) sterilization
   c) sanitation
   d) disinfection
   _____

3. A very important part of a pleasing personality is a good:
   a) financial standing
   b) list of stories
   c) loud voice
   d) sense of humor
   _____

4. Proper conduct in relation to employer, clients, and coworkers is called professional:
   a) personality
   b) ethics
   c) courtesy
   d) honesty
   _____

5. Bacteria live and grow best in:
   a) cold places
   b) dry places
   c) dirty places
   d) clean places
   _____

6. A wet sanitizer should contain:
   a) a disinfectant solution
   b) 30% alcohol
   c) an antiseptic solution
   d) 2% formalin
   _____

7. A quaternary ammonium compound is commonly used as a/an:
   a) disinfectant
   b) styptic
   c) antiseptic
   d) deodorant
   _____

8. A method used to keep disinfected objects sanitary is:
   a) germicide
   b) wrap in plastic wrap
   c) disinfectant
   d) sepsis
   _____

9. Creams are removed from jars with:
   a) the end of a used towel
   b) the tips of fingers
   c) a clean spatula
   d) a used orangewood stick
   _____

10. The largest organ of the human body is the:
    a) heart
    b) lungs
    c) skin
    d) stomach
    _____

11. The outer protective layer of the skin is called the:
    a) dermis
    b) adipose tissue
    c) epidermis
    d) subcutaneous tissue
    _____

12. The hair takes its shape, size, and direction from its:
    a) cortex   c) medulla
    b) cuticle   d) follicle   ____

13. The hair cuticle is the:
    a) pith   c) second layer
    b) outer layer   d) marrow   ____

14. Itching is an example of a/an:
    a) subjective symptom   c) primary skin lesion
    b) objective symptom   d) secondary skin lesion ____

15. Comedone is the technical name for a:
    a) whitehead   c) blackhead
    b) pimple   d) dry skin   ____

16. Dandruff is generally believed to be:
    a) an allergy   c) noncontagious
    b) nonpathogenic   d) infectious   ____

17. Alopecia is the technical term for any abnormal form of:
    a) hair loss   c) oil gland disorder
    b) skin inflammation   d) sweat gland disorder ____

18. During the shampoo, a scalp massage is given with:
    a) the cushions of the   c) rubber gloves
       fingertips
    b) the metacarpus   d) ear pads   ____

19. Hair lightening involves the:
    a) diffusing of natural   c) restoring gray hair to
       pigment from the hair   its original color
    b) adding artificial pigment   d) adding artificial pigment
       to the natural hair color   to a prelightened hair ____

20. Nonstrip shampoos are recommended for hair that is:
    a) normal   c) tinted
    b) coarse   d) oily   ____

21. Permanent haircoloring tints are mixed with:
    a) sodium hydroxide   c) formalin
    b) sodium bromate   d) hydrogen peroxide ____

22. The first consideration of the cosmetologist always should be
    the:
    a) fee to be charged   c) time consumed
    b) protection of the client   d) client's tips   ____

23. The neck strip or towel is used to prevent:
    a) the client from   c) complete saturation
       perspiring   of the hair
    b) the cape from touching   d) an unpleasant feeling
       the skin   to the client   ____

24. A rinse that is formulated to make tangled hair easier to comb is a:
    a) medicated rinse
    b) reconditioned rinse
    c) nonstrip rinse
    d) cream rinse
    _____

25. A rinse that is designed to highlight the color of the hair is a/an:
    a) cream rinse
    b) tartaric rinse
    c) color rinse
    d) acid rinse
    _____

26. The hair must be damp if hair thinning is done with:
    a) shears
    b) clippers
    c) a razor
    d) thinning scissors
    _____

27. The choice of setting lotion should be determined by:
    a) its drying qualities
    b) its color
    c) the texture of client's hair
    d) its lacquer consistency
    _____

28. Hair that can be thinned closest to the scalp is:
    a) fine
    b) medium
    c) coarse
    d) damaged
    _____

29. If bangs are to be cut, it is important to test the hair for:
    a) oiliness
    b) ratting
    c) bounce
    d) color
    _____

30. The best results in finger waving are obtained when the hair is:
    a) straight
    b) naturally wavy
    c) frizzy
    d) kinky
    _____

31. A good finger-waving lotion:
    a) dries very slowly
    b) colors the hair
    c) is harmless to the hair
    d) lightens the hair
    _____

32. A safe antiseptic to cleanse the skin is:
    a) 3% hydrogen peroxide
    b) hydrochloric acid
    c) carbolic acid
    d) bichloride of mercury
    _____

33. The process of removing tangles from the hair should start in the:
    a) crown area
    b) hairline area
    c) nape area
    d) forehead area
    _____

34. The immovable part of the curl attached to the scalp is the:
    a) stem
    b) base
    c) circle
    d) arc
    _____

35. The mobility of a pin curl is determined by its:
    a) base
    b) stem
    c) pivot
    d) circle
    _____

36. The four most common curl bases used in hairstyling are the square base, rectangular base, triangular base, and:
    a) circular base
    b) flat base
    c) arc or half-moon base
    d) elevated base
    _____

37. To avoid splits or breaks at the front or facial hairline, use:
   a) triangular bases
   b) square bases
   c) circular bases
   d) round bases
   ____

38. A wave formed by alternating finger waves and pin curls is called a:
   a) loose wave
   b) standup wave
   c) skip wave
   d) full wave
   ____

39. When styling a wig, pin curls are used instead of rollers to keep the:
   a) fibers from unraveling
   b) fullness of the style
   c) style close to the head
   d) hair tightly knotted
   ____

40. Presoftening before applying a one-step (one-process) hair tint serves to:
   a) remove metallic dye
   b) soften lightened hair
   c) harden lightened hair
   d) decrease the resistance of hair
   ____

41. Haircolor rinses are colorings that are:
   a) permanent
   b) temporary
   c) semipermanent
   d) penetrating
   ____

42. The natural color of hair, whether dark or light, is determined by its:
   a) cuticle
   b) texture
   c) medulla
   d) pigment
   ____

43. When matching hair color, the hair nearest the scalp at the back of the head is found to be the:
   a) lightest
   b) longest
   c) darkest
   d) shortest
   ____

44. Aniline derivative tints:
   a) penetrate the hair shaft
   b) harden the hair shaft
   c) coat the hair shaft
   d) highlight the hair shaft
   ____

45. Color shades with some red or gold tones are classified as being:
   a) drab
   b) warm
   c) silver
   d) cool
   ____

46. Vigorously brushing the hair before a permanent wave may cause:
   a) hair discoloration
   b) scalp tightening
   c) healthy hair to fall out
   d) scalp irritations
   ____

47. The main ingredient in cold-waving solution or lotion is:
   a) aniline derivative
   b) sodium hydroxide
   c) ammonium thioglycolate
   d) hydrogen peroxide
   ____

48. If too much tension is used when wrapping the hair, the action of the permanent-wave solution could be:
   a) retarded
   b) hastened
   c) stopped
   d) accelerated
   ____

49. In acid-balanced or neutral permanent waving, damage to the hair is minimized because:

   a) waving lotion is used
   b) concentrated heat is applied
   c) harsh alkalis are not used
   d) permanent-wave rods are used _____

50. Acid-balanced permanent waving is done without offensive odors because:

   a) the processing is very fast
   b) heat neutralizes the odor
   c) the solution is highly perfumed
   d) no ammonia is used _____

51. The main purpose of a hair and scalp treatment is to:

   a) cure canities
   b) harden the texture of hair
   c) preserve the health of hair and scalp
   d) preserve the color of hair _____

52. After a scalp cream has been applied, expose the scalp to:

   a) ultraviolet rays
   b) heat rays
   c) rays of blue lights
   d) actinic rays _____

53. The technique of drying and styling damp hair in one operation is called:

   a) croquignole styling
   b) thermal irons styling
   c) thermal styling
   d) blow-dry styling _____

54. When in operation, the blow-dryer produces a steady stream of temperature-controlled:

   a) vapors
   b) air
   c) water
   d) steam _____

55. Before attempting to comb out blow-dried hair, it must be thoroughly:

   a) brushed
   b) tangled
   c) cooled
   d) permed _____

56. The action of the chemical hair relaxer causes the hair to:

   a) soften and swell
   b) form new curls
   c) harden and set
   d) shrink _____

57. The chemical relaxing cream is applied to the scalp area last because the processing is speeded up in this area by:

   a) the accelerator
   b) 10% ammonia
   c) body heat
   d) hydrogen peroxide _____

58. The two methods of chemical hair relaxing are the thio method and the:

   a) thermal method
   b) sodium hydroxide method
   c) single-process method
   d) gentian violet method _____

59. In permanent waving, a test curl serves as a guide to determine the:
   a) neutralizing time
   b) size of hair sections
   c) processing time
   d) amount of tension to be used ____

60. The temperature of the pressing comb should be adjusted to the hair's:
   a) cleanliness
   b) shortness
   c) texture
   d) length ____

61. Hair that appears lifeless and limp is usually lacking in:
   a) elasticity
   b) texture
   c) porosity
   d) density ____

62. Electric vaporizing irons should not be used on pressed hair because they cause the hair to:
   a) revert
   b) break
   c) straighten
   d) discolor ____

63. Eye shadow is usually applied to the:
   a) eyelashes
   b) eyebrows
   c) eyelids
   d) mouth ____

64. The nail is composed of a substance called:
   a) melanin
   b) hemoglobin
   c) keratin
   d) corpuscles ____

65. The deep fold of skin in which the nail root is lodged is called the:
   a) mantle
   b) nail groove
   c) nail wall
   d) nail bed ____

66. Brittle nails and dry cuticles are treated with a/an:
   a) oil manicure
   b) top sealer
   c) regular manicure
   d) machine manicure ____

67. Minor bleeding in manicuring is stopped with:
   a) alcohol
   b) acetone
   c) alum
   d) a sealer ____

68. Blisters and skin irritation between the toes are signs of:
   a) pterygium
   b) onychia
   c) pedicuring
   d) athlete's foot ____

69. To prevent or correct brittle nails and dry cuticles, use:
   a) nail whitener
   b) cuticle solvent
   c) cuticle cream
   d) dry nail polish ____

70. In massage, the effects of effleurage are:
   a) stimulating
   b) soothing and relaxing
   c) invigorating
   d) magnetic ____

71. The immediate effects of massage are first noticed:
    a) in the mucous membranes
    b) inside the mouth
    c) on the skin
    d) under the eyelids ____

72. When giving a facial, eye pads should be applied before using:
    a) massage manipulations
    b) astringent lotion
    c) foundation cream
    d) red dermal light ____

73. A person who has naturally light-colored hair has in their hair:
    a) great amounts of large melanin molecules
    b) lesser amounts of small melanin molecules
    c) an abundance of dark melanin molecules
    d) only large melanin molecules ____

74. A hot oil mask is recommended for skin that is:
    a) oily
    b) dry
    c) tanned
    d) freckled ____

75. Before applying a chemical depilatory, it is necessary to give a/an:
    a) hair test
    b) strand test
    c) skin test
    d) acid test ____

76. In corrective makeup, use a lighter shade than the foundation to:
    a) decrease the size of features
    b) produce a shadow effect
    c) make prominent features less noticeable
    d) produce a highlight effect ____

77. Lip color is applied to a client's lips:
    a) with a used orangewood stick
    b) with a sanitized lip brush
    c) with your fingers
    d) directly from the lipstick tube ____

78. To correct misshaped and uneven eyebrows, it is best to use a/an:
    a) electric clipper
    b) straight razor
    c) eyebrow pencil
    d) depilatory ____

79. The process of affixing semipermanent individual eyelashes is referred to as:
    a) stripping
    b) eye tabbing
    c) adhesive lashes
    d) brush lashes ____

80. In addition to eye tabbing, another type of false eyelashes is:
    a) individual eyelashes
    b) strip lashes
    c) semipermanent lashes
    d) adhesive lashes ____

81. A constant and direct current used to produce chemical effects on the tissues and fluids of the body is the:
    a) faradic current
    b) sinusoidal current
    c) Tesla current
    d) galvanic current ____

82. A glass electrode that gives off sparks operates on:
   a) galvanic current
   b) faradic current
   c) sinusoidal current
   d) high-frequency current ____

83. The shortest and least penetrating light rays of the spectrum are the:
   a) infrared rays
   b) ultraviolet rays
   c) orange light rays
   d) red light rays ____

84. The shorter rays reach the skin when the ultraviolet ray lamp is placed within:
   a) 36" from body
   b) 12" from body
   c) 30" from body
   d) 40" from body ____

85. Natural hair color is created by the reflection or _____ of light rays by melanin.
   a) disintegration
   b) segregation
   c) absorption
   d) reduction ____

86. An alteration of the properties of a substance without the formation of any new substance is a:
   a) mixture
   b) chemical change
   c) compound
   d) physical change ____

87. Removing impurities from water by passing it through a porous substance is the process of:
   a) distillation
   b) neutralization
   c) filtration
   d) oxidation ____

88. A preparation made by dissolving a solid, liquid, or gaseous substance in another substance is a/an:
   a) suspension
   b) ointment
   c) solution
   d) powder ____

89. A good location for a beauty salon is near a:
   a) supermarket
   b) machine shop
   c) bowling alley
   d) tavern ____

90. The best form of advertising is a:
   a) neon sign
   b) pleased client
   c) newspaper ad
   d) window pane ____

91. Business neglect and careless bookkeeping often result in salon:
   a) growth
   b) success
   c) failure
   d) development ____

92. Good telephone habits and techniques help to build up the salon's:
   a) reputation
   b) appearance
   c) location
   d) gossip ____

93. The first step in successful selling in the beauty salon is to:
   a) break down resistance
   b) discourage competition
   c) sell yourself
   d) be aggressive ____

94. Maintaining a simple but efficient record-keeping system is a requirement of good:
    a) customer relations
    b) sales control
    c) sale of services
    d) business administration   ____

95. In manicuring, if the cuticle is cut or broken, it is advisable to apply a/an:
    a) disinfectant
    b) antiseptic
    c) caustic
    d) sodium   ____

96. The nucleus of the cell controls its:
    a) excretions
    b) self-repair
    c) secretions
    d) reproduction   ____

97. The skeletal system is important because it:
    a) covers and shapes the body
    b) supplies the body with blood
    c) is the physical foundation of the body
    d) carries nerve messages   ____

98. Muscles controlled by the will are called:
    a) involuntary muscles
    b) voluntary muscles
    c) cardiac muscles
    d) nonstriated muscles   ____

99. The nervous system is composed of the brain and spinal cord and their:
    a) blood vessels
    b) nerves
    c) lymphatics
    d) glands   ____

100. Vessels that carry blood away from the heart are called:
    a) veins
    b) arteries
    c) capillaries
    d) lymphatics   ____

TYPICAL STATE BOARD EXAMINATIONS
TEST 2–100 MULTIPLE CHOICE QUESTIONS

DIRECTIONS: *Carefully read each statement. Choose the word or phrase that correctly completes the meaning of each statement and write the most correct corresponding letter on top of line.*

1. An important attribute of good professional ethics is:
   a) temper
   b) loyalty
   c) arrogance
   d) gossip
   _____

2. The use of good speech is vital to the art of:
   a) literature
   b) fashion
   c) conversation
   d) grooming
   _____

3. Personal hygiene deals with the preservation of the well-being of the:
   a) individual
   b) community
   c) town
   d) society
   _____

4. Body odors can be prevented by regular bathing and the use of:
   a) styptics
   b) astringents
   c) vapors
   d) deodorants
   _____

5. Sharp metallic instruments may be sanitized with:
   a) 30% alcohol
   b) 50% alcohol
   c) 70% alcohol
   d) 40% alcohol
   _____

6. A covered receptacle containing a disinfectant solution is a/an:
   a) dry sanitizer
   b) cabinet sanitizer
   c) wet sanitizer
   d) oven sanitizer
   _____

7. As a disinfectant, a quarternary ammonium compound is considered to be:
   a) corrosive
   b) toxic
   c) unstable
   d) odorless
   _____

8. When a sanitized comb is not in use, it should be kept in a:
   a) uniform pocket
   b) dry sanitizer
   c) dresser drawer
   d) fumigant solution
   _____

9. Pathogenic bacteria are commonly known as:
   a) antiseptics
   b) disinfectants
   c) germs
   d) beneficial bacteria
   _____

10. Hair is chiefly composed of a horny substance called:
    a) hemoglobin
    b) melanin
    c) keratin
    d) calcium
    _____

11. Hair strength and elasticity are traceable to the:
    a) medulla
    b) cuticle
    c) follicle
    d) cortex
    _____

12. A healthy skin should be:
    a) perfectly dry
    b) without any color
    c) slightly moist and soft
    d) bluish in color   ____

13. The skin is thinnest on the:
    a) eyebrows
    b) eyelids
    c) forehead
    d) backs of the hands   ____

14. Long-neglected dandruff may lead to:
    a) tinea
    b) scabies
    c) baldness
    d) psoriasis   ____

15. Baldness in spots is known as alopecia:
    a) adnata
    b) senilis
    c) areata
    d) dynamica   ____

16. Acne is a disorder of the:
    a) sweat glands
    b) oil glands
    c) intestinal glands
    d) stomach glands   ____

17. A papule is a:
    a) secondary skin lesion
    b) primary skin lesion
    c) tertiary skin lesion
    d) subjective symptom   ____

18. When an acid rinse has been used, it is followed with a:
    a) clear warm-water rinse
    b) soapless oil shampoo
    c) dry shampoo
    d) bluing rinse   ____

19. A rinse formulated to prevent the removal of color from the hair
    is a:
    a) vinegar rinse
    b) lemon rinse
    c) bluing rinse
    d) nonstrip rinse   ____

20. In protecting the client's skin and clothing, proper draping is
    considered to be:
    a) an extra service
    b) a glamorous service
    c) completely unnecessary
    d) the first line of protection   ____

21. The personal factor that contributes most to bringing clients back
    to the salon is the cosmetologist's:
    a) aggressiveness
    b) familiarity
    c) gossip
    d) personality   ____

22. Strongly alkaline shampoos make the hair:
    a) soft and silky
    b) dry and brittle
    c) color fast
    d) easier to comb   ____

23. After a regular shampoo, rinse away all the soap from the hair
    with:
    a) a cream rinse
    b) cold water
    c) hot water
    d) lukewarm water   ____

24. The main active ingredient in acid-balanced waving lotion is:
    a) glyceryl monothioglycolate
    b) ammonium thioglycolate
    c) sodium hydroxide
    d) hydrogen peroxide   ____

25. Brushing the hair as part of the shampoo or scalp treatment:
    a) damages the scalp
    b) tangles the hair
    c) stimulates circulation
    d) irritates the scalp ____

26. When giving a finger wave, what makes the hair more pliable and holds it in place?
    a) a cream rinse
    b) setting lotion
    c) hair lacquer
    d) a neutralizer ____

27. Before finger waving locate the:
    a) new hair growth
    b) receding hairline
    c) natural wave
    d) line of demarcation ____

28. For a hairstyle with a side part, the finger wave should be started on the:
    a) thin side of the hair
    b) back of the head
    c) heavy side of the hair
    d) crown part of the head ____

29. The type of hair that is best for pin curling is:
    a) straight, coarse hair
    b) natural or permanent-waved hair
    c) fine curly hair
    d) wiry, overcurly hair ____

30. The part of a pin curl found between the base and the first arc of the circle is known as the:
    a) circle
    b) stem
    c) pivot
    d) strand ____

31. A firm, immovable position, permitting only the circle of the curl to move, is created by a:
    a) no-stem curl
    b) half-stem curl
    c) full-stem curl
    d) round-stem curl ____

32. The stabilizer is also known as neutralizer or:
    a) thio
    b) caustic
    c) ammonium
    d) fixative ____

33. A strand of hair wound in circles within a circle is called a:
    a) curl
    b) shaping
    c) ridge
    d) section ____

34. Pin curls that are placed behind the ridgeline of a shaping are called:
    a) roller curls
    b) ridge curls
    c) pivot curls
    d) finger curls ____

35. Human hair wigs may be properly cleansed by:
    a) drycleaning
    b) a shampoo tint
    c) an alkaline soap
    d) sodium hydroxide ____

36. Coarse hair should never be thinned close to the:
    a) sides
    b) hair shaft
    c) cuticle
    d) scalp ____

37. The thinning of hair involves:
    a) cutting it straight off
    b) blunt cutting
    c) decreasing its bulk
    d) trimming the ends ____

38. If the hair is thinned near the ends of the strands, it will be:
    a) shapeless
    b) slithered
    c) blunt cut
    d) shingled ____

39. A finger wave lasts longer when the hair is molded:
    a) in very high ridges
    b) in the direction of
       the natural growth
    c) in very low ridges
    d) opposite to the inclination
       of natural growth ____

40. One method of wrapping a permanent wave with extra long hair is the:
    a) double halo method
    b) piggyback method
    c) dropped crown method
    d) single halo method ____

41. If permanent waving, a longer processing time is usually required for hair that is:
    a) lightened
    b) tinted
    c) porous
    d) resistant ____

42. If the fastening band is twisted or stretched too tightly in permanent waving, it may cause a:
    a) frizzy curl
    b) springy curl
    c) breakage of hair
    d) resilient curl ____

43. Since there is little hair swelling in acid-balanced permanent waving, there is only a minimum of hair:
    a) curling
    b) breakage
    c) penetration
    d) perming ____

44. Since no ammonia is used in acid-balanced permanent waving, there is less chance of:
    a) skin irritation
    b) color control
    c) penetration of the lotion
    d) soft, natural-looking
       waves ____

45. A temporary haircoloring used to add color to the eyelashes is:
    a) certified color
    b) aniline
    c) mascara
    d) mineral dye ____

46. The hair tint that colors and lightens the hair several shades in one application is the:
    a) two-process tint
    b) metallic dye
    c) two-step tint
    d) single-process tint ____

47. Eyebrows should be properly tweezed in the direction:
    a) opposite to their
       natural growth
    b) of their natural growth
    c) toward the chin
    d) toward the scalp ____

48. When the desired shade is reached, the lightener should be removed with:
    a) sulfonated oil
    b) cool water
    c) hydrogen peroxide
    d) hot water ____

49. Color shades with no red are classified as being:
    a) warm
    b) rich
    c) cool
    d) very warm ____

50. The best time to prepare the hair lightening formula is:
    a) a day before using it
    b) a week before using it
    c) immediately before using it
    d) two days before using it ____

51. An electrical device especially designed for drying and styling the hair in a single operation is a:
    a) thermal dryer
    b) hood dryer
    c) blow dryer
    d) curl dryer ____

52. Excessive hairstyling by the blow-drying may cause dryness and:
    a) deep waves
    b) split ends
    c) discoloration
    d) shadow waves ____

53. The styling of hair with an air waver is performed in the same manner as:
    a) thermal waving
    b) blow-out waving
    c) chemical waving
    d) finger waving ____

54. Scalp massage is beneficial because it stimulates the:
    a) salivary gland
    b) blood circulation
    c) pituitary gland
    d) thyroid gland ____

55. An essential part of a scalp treatment is:
    a) scalp tightening
    b) combing of hair
    c) hair brushing
    d) color rinsing ____

56. Overheated irons often are ruined because the metal loses its:
    a) color
    b) balance
    c) temper
    d) shape ____

57. The thermal iron curl that provides a strong curl with full volume is the:
    a) half-base curl
    b) full-base curl
    c) off-base curl
    d) no-base curl ____

58. In order to maintain accurate and efficient control of supplies, it is necessary to have an organized:
    a) inventory system
    b) purchase order
    c) sales force
    d) depreciation record ____

59. A double treatment with a heated comb is known as a:
    a) soft press
    b) hard press
    c) regular press
    d) comb press ____

60. The process of straightening overcurly hair by the use of chemical agents is known as chemical hair:
    a) neutralizing   c) relaxing
    b) stabilizing   d) stranding   ____

61. If a chemical relaxer is applied to hair that has been hot-comb treated, it could result in:
    a) tangled hair   c) hair breakage
    b) stabilization   d) curl reversion   ____

62. Before a chemical relaxing treatment, take a:
    a) strand test   c) stabilizing test
    b) filler test   d) patch test   ____

63. When performing a chemical blow-out, the important consideration is that the hair is not:
    a) blow dried   c) underrelaxed
    b) overrelaxed   d lifted   ____

64. To help prevent dry skin around the nails, apply:
    a) cuticle cream   c) alcohol
    b) nail polish remover   d) an antiseptic   ____

65. A cosmetic applied over the nail polish to minimize chipping or cracking is a/an:
    a) base coat   c) lacquer
    b) sealer   d) abrasive   ____

66. The nail plate starts from the nail root and extends to the:
    a) lunula   c) nail bed
    b) nail matrix   d) free edge   ____

67. The lunula is the visible half-moon area at the nail's:
    a) edge   c) base
    b) nail matrix   d) groove   ____

68. Another name for athlete's foot is:
    a) varicose   c) ringworm
    b) pityriasis   d) pterygium   ____

69. To soften and lubricate the skin around the nails, apply:
    a) pumice powder   c) cuticle solvent
    b) nail bleach   d) cuticle oil   ____

70. The sanitized end of a comedone extractor is used to remove:
    a) blackheads   c) freckles
    b) moles   d) birthmarks   ____

71. After the massage cream has been removed, the face should be sponged with a/an:
    a) caustic lotion   c) setting lotion
    b) disinfectant lotion   d) astringent lotion   ____

72. Blackheads are formed by a hardened mass of sebum in the ducts of the:
   a) thyroid gland
   b) salivary glands
   c) sebaceous gland
   d) sudoriferous glands ____

73. Petrissage is what type of massage movement?
   a) friction
   b) percussion
   c) tapotement
   d) kneading ____

74. Firm kneading massage movements usually produce what sensation to body tissues?
   a) stimulation
   b) coolness
   c) soothing
   d) relaxation ____

75. Hair may be temporarily removed by:
   a) diathermy
   b) depilatories
   c) shortwaves
   d) galvanic current ____

76. Applying hot cotton over the eyebrows before tweezing tends to:
   a) make it more painful
   b) soften and relax eyebrows
   c) tighten the tissues
   d) contract the skin ____

77. Before applying individual lashes, it is advisable to give a/an:
   a) color test
   b) endurance test
   c) strand test
   d) allergy test ____

78. False eyelashes will not hold as long on clients with:
   a) sparse eyelashes
   b) cemented eyelashes
   c) eye tabbing
   d) oily eyelids ____

79. Face powder should:
   a) be several shades darker than the foundation
   b) match or coordinate with the foundation
   c) be several shades lighter than the foundation
   d) be eliminated when foundation is used ____

80. To make the eyes look larger and lashes appear thicker, apply:
   a) eye shadow
   b) eyeliners
   c) eye cream
   d) cheek color ____

81. About 80% of natural sunshine consists of:
   a) ultraviolet rays
   b) actinic rays
   c) visible light rays
   d) infrared rays ____

82. Both the cosmetologist and client must wear eye safety glasses to protect their eyes when exposed to:
   a) violet rays
   b) ultraviolet rays
   c) white dermal light
   d) red dermal light ____

83. A substance that readily transmits an electric current is known as a/an:
   a) conductor
   b) nonconductor
   c) insulator
   d) converter ____

84. An alternating and interrupted current, used principally to cause muscular contractions, is the:
   a) faradic current
   b) high-frequency current
   c) Tesla current
   d) galvanic current
   ____

85. A soap solution with a pH factor of 10 would be considered to be a/an:
   a) acid
   b) salt
   c) alkali
   d) oxide
   ____

86. The most abundant element is:
   a) oxygen
   b) hydrogen
   c) nitrogen
   d) ammonia
   ____

87. Cosmetologists repeating gossip will cause loss of the client's:
   a) attention
   b) charm
   c) confidence
   d) posture
   ____

88. To avoid splits when using square bases, it is advisable to:
   a) stagger the sectioning
   b) overlap the bases
   c) use a French twist
   d) use uniform curls
   ____

89. Smooth salon operations are usually the result of:
   a) efficient management
   b) insufficient capital
   c) business neglect
   d) careless controls
   ____

90. Keeping accurate daily records permits salon management to evaluate:
   a) employee relations
   b) business progress
   c) customer relations
   d) appointments
   ____

91. Building maintenance and renovations are regulated by:
   a) federal laws
   b) local ordinances
   c) state laws
   d) interstate regulations
   ____

92. The first medium to be used for salon advertising is the:
   a) radio
   b) television
   c) newspaper
   d) billboard
   ____

93. Salon business can be promoted effectively over the telephone, provided there is:
   a) time to waste
   b) business neglect
   c) good planning
   d) sufficient capital
   ____

94. In order to make selling agreeable and productive, the cosmetologist must be:
   a) self-confident
   b) impatient
   c) overbearing
   d) ingratiating
   ____

95. A chronic inflammatory congestion of the cheeks and nose characterized by redness and dilation of the blood vessels is called:
   a) milia
   b) asteatosis
   c) seborrhea
   d) rosacea
   ____

96. Cells are the basic units of:
    a) dead matter
    b) living matter
    c) chemicals
    d) cosmetics ____

97. The more fixed attachment of a muscle is called:
    a) origin of muscle
    b) insertion of muscle
    c) muscle tone
    d) ligament ____

98. The nervous system controls and coordinates all body:
    a) structures
    b) functions
    c) diseases
    d) cleanliness ____

99. The fluid part of the blood is called:
    a) plasma
    b) white blood cells
    c) red blood cells
    d) thrombocytes ____

100. An important function of bone is to:
    a) create calcium
    b) protect the body
       organs
    c) stimulate the muscles
    d) stimulate blood
       circulation ____

A removable answer
key follows this page

Answers to
State Exam Review
for Cosmetology

ANSWERS
TO
STATE EXAM REVIEW FOR
COSMETOLOGY

YOUR PROFESSIONAL IMAGE

1—b	9—b	17—a	25—a	33—d	41—b	49—c
2—c	10—d	18—c	26—d	34—b	42—b	50—d
3—a	11—d	19—d	27—c	35—d	43—a	51—d
4—c	12—a	20—c	28—d	36—d	44—d	52—c
5—c	13—b	21—c	29—a	37—d	45—c	53—c
6—c	14—b	22—b	30—b	38—c	46—b	54—d
7—b	15—a	23—c	31—c	39—d	47—c	55—b
8—d	16—b	24—b	32—c	40—b	48—b	56—a

BACTERIOLOGY

1—c	5—b	9—a	13—b	17—c	21—b	25—c
2—b	6—c	10—c	14—c	18—b	22—b	26—a
3—c	7—c	11—b	15—a	19—b	23—d	27—d
4—b	8—a	12—a	16—b	20—c	24—a	

DECONTAMINATION AND INFECTION CONTROL

1—c	6—c	11—b	16—c	21—a	26—a	31—c
2—b	7—a	12—a	17—b	22—c	27—b	32—a
3—a	8—b	13—c	18—d	23—b	28—c	33—c
4—d	9—d	14—a	19—c	24—d	29—d	34—d
5—b	10—c	15—b	20—b	25—c	30—b	35—a

PROPERTIES OF THE HAIR AND SCALP

1—c	16—a	31—d	46—c	61—a	76—c	91—a
2—b	17—b	32—b	47—a	62—c	77—c	92—c
3—c	18—c	33—b	48—d	63—c	78—b	93—a
4—b	19—d	34—c	49—b	64—b	79—d	94—b
5—d	20—c	35—d	50—a	65—c	80—c	95—c
6—c	21—c	36—b	51—b	66—d	81—b	96—c
7—a	22—d	37—d	52—d	67—b	82—c	97—b
8—c	23—c	38—c	53—c	68—c	83—b	98—a
9—b	24—b	39—a	54—d	69—a	84—b	99—a
10—c	25—b	40—d	55—c	70—b	85—a	100—b
11—a	26—c	41—b	56—d	71—d	86—b	101—c
12—d	27—b	42—c	57—c	72—d	87—c	102—b
13—d	28—c	43—a	58—d	73—c	88—d	
14—a	29—c	44—b	59—b	74—c	89—b	
15—a	30—a	45—d	60—a	75—b	90—a	

DRAPING

1—b	3—d	5—a	7—b	9—b	11—d
2—c	4—d	6—b	8—c	10—a	

SHAMPOOING, RINSING, AND CONDITIONING

1—b	5—d	9—a	13—b	17—a	21—d	25—c
2—c	6—a	10—c	14—c	18—a	22—b	
3—b	7—a	11—b	15—b	19—b	23—b	
4—a	8—a	12—c	16—a	20—d	24—d	

2

HAIRCUTTING

1—c	4—c	7—d	10—b	13—a	16—d	19—b
2—d	5—c	8—c	11—b	14—c	17—a	20—d
3—a	6—d	9—c	12—c	15—a	18—d	21—b

FINGER WAVING

1—b	4—c	7—d	10—b	13—a	15—c
2—d	5—c	8—a	11—a	14—c	16—b
3—b	6—c	9—c	12—c		

WET HAIRSTYLING

1—c	8—c	15—a	22—a	29—b	36—c	43—a
2—d	9—b	16—b	23—c	30—a	37—c	44—b
3—c	10—b	17—a	24—d	31—b	38—a	45—d
4—d	11—d	18—a	25—c	32—c	39—d	46—b
5—b	12—a	19—d	26—c	33—b	40—c	47—d
6—b	13—b	20—b	27—c	34—a	41—c	
7—b	14—c	21—b	28—a	35—b	42—d	

THERMAL HAIRSTYLING

1—b	6—b	11—d	16—c	21—b	26—c	29—d
2—a	7—c	12—c	17—b	22—a	27—d	30—a
3—c	8—b	13—b	18—a	23—b	28—d	
4—d	9—c	14—c	19—d	24—b		
5—b	10—b	15—d	20—c	25—a		

PERMANENT WAVING

1—d	9—a	17—a	25—b	33—c	41—b	49—a
2—a	10—b	18—c	26—c	34—c	42—b	50—d
3—c	11—c	19—a	27—c	35—c	43—b	51—b
4—b	12—d	20—a	28—d	36—c	44—c	52—c
5—d	13—c	21—c	29—d	37—b	45—c	
6—b	14—b	22—a	30—a	38—d	46—b	
7—d	15—d	23—a	31—b	39—d	47—d	
8—d	16—b	24—b	32—c	40—a	48—d	

HAIR COLORING

1—c	18—c	35—a	52—a	69—d	86—d	103—b
2—d	19—b	36—b	53—b	70—b	87—a	104—c
3—a	20—a	37—c	54—b	71—b	88—b	105—a
4—b	21—b	38—d	55—b	72—c	89—c	106—a
5—d	22—a	39—b	56—d	73—b	90—c	107—c
6—b	23—c	40—a	57—a	74—c	91—d	108—c
7—c	24—b	41—c	58—b	75—b	92—b	109—a
8—d	25—c	42—a	59—c	76—b	93—a	110—c
9—a	26—b	43—b	60—b	77—a	94—b	111—a
10—c	27—c	44—a	61—a	78—a	95—b	112—b
11—a	28—d	45—c	62—a	79—b	96—b	113—c
12—a	29—a	46—a	63—b	80—b	97—d	114—a
13—d	30—c	47—c	64—d	81—b	98—c	115—d
14—b	31—b	48—d	65—c	82—d	99—b	116—b
15—a	32—a	49—c	66—d	83—b	100—b	117—d
16—c	33—d	50—c	67—c	84—c	101—c	
17—d	34—c	51—c	68—b	85—b	102—d	

CHEMICAL HAIR RELAXING AND SOFT-CURL PERMANENT

1—c	6—d	11—b	16—b	21—c	26—a	31—a
2—a	7—d	12—c	17—b	22—c	27—c	32—b
3—d	8—b	13—b	18—d	23—b	28—a	
4—d	9—d	14—a	19—b	24—d	29—a	
5—b	10—c	15—d	20—a	25—b	30—c	

THERMAL HAIR STRAIGHTENING

1—d	6—a	11—b	16—d	21—b	26—d	31—c
2—c	7—b	12—b	17—b	22—a	27—d	32—a
3—b	8—c	13—b	18—c	23—b	28—d	33—c
4—d	9—b	14—b	19—a	24—b	29—c	34—b
5—b	10—c	15—b	20—c	25—b	30—b	

THE ARTISTRY OF ARTIFICIAL HAIR

1—c	3—b	5—a	7—b	9—d	11—a	13—c
2—d	4—a	6—c	8—c	10—b	12—c	

MANICURING AND PEDICURING

1—c	7—a	13—d	19—a	25—d	31—c	37—b
2—b	8—b	14—b	20—a	26—c	32—d	38—b
3—c	9—a	15—c	21—c	27—d	33—b	39—c
4—a	10—a	16—b	22—d	28—c	34—d	40—b
5—c	11—c	17—c	23—a	29—a	35—a	41—b
6—b	12—a	18—d	24—a	30—c	36—c	42—c

THE NAIL AND ITS DISORDERS

1—a	8—b	15—b	22—d	29—c	36—c	43—c
2—b	9—b	16—b	23—a	30—c	37—c	44—c
3—d	10—a	17—b	24—d	31—c	38—c	45—b
4—c	11—c	18—c	25—a	32—d	39—a	46—b
5—b	12—b	19—b	26—b	33—b	40—c	47—b
6—c	13—b	20—d	27—c	34—b	41—b	48—a
7—d	14—c	21—a	28—c	35—a	42—b	49—d

THEORY OF MASSAGE

1—d	3—d	5—c	7—c	9—a	11—c
2—b	4—c	6—d	8—d	10—d	12—b

FACIALS

1—c	5—d	9—b	13—b	17—d	21—c
2—d	6—b	10—c	14—a	18—c	22—d
3—a	7—d	11—d	15—b	19—c	
4—c	8—c	12—c	16—b	20—b	

FACIAL MAKEUP

1—d	6—b	11—b	16—b	21—b	26—d	29—c
2—d	7—a	12—c	17—c	22—d	27—a	30—b
3—b	8—b	13—c	18—b	23—a	28—d	
4—a	9—a	14—b	19—a	24—b		
5—d	10—d	15—b	20—b	25—d		

4

THE SKIN AND ITS DISORDERS

1—c	15—b	29—b	43—c	57—b	71—c	85—b
2—c	16—c	30—b	44—d	58—d	72—c	86—b
3—b	17—b	31—b	45—c	59—c	73—c	87—a
4—b	18—b	32—a	46—d	60—a	74—b	88—d
5—a	19—b	33—b	47—a	61—b	75—c	89—d
6—b	20—b	34—b	48—d	62—c	76—d	90—b
7—c	21—d	35—c	49—b	63—a	77—d	91—b
8—d	22—b	36—c	50—b	64—a	78—c	92—c
9—b	23—b	37—d	51—d	65—c	79—b	93—b
10—b	24—d	38—d	52—b	66—c	80—c	94—c
11—b	25—c	39—b	53—c	67—c	81—a	95—b
12—b	26—c	40—c	54—b	68—c	82—d	96—c
13—c	27—a	41—c	55—c	69—a	83—b	97—c
14—b	28—c	42—b	56—a	70—b	84—b	98—a

REMOVING UNWANTED HAIR

1—d	4—b	7—a	10—c	13—c	16—c	19—a
2—c	5—b	8—b	11—b	14—d	17—c	20—c
3—a	6—d	9—d	12—d	15—d	18—a	21—d

CELLS, ANATOMY, AND PHYSIOLOGY

1—b	19—a	37—c	55—b	73—b	91—a	109—b
2—a	20—b	38—c	56—b	74—b	92—c	110—d
3—c	21—c	39—a	57—d	75—c	93—a	111—a
4—d	22—c	40—a	58—c	76—b	94—c	112—c
5—b	23—d	41—b	59—d	77—a	95—b	113—a
6—d	24—d	42—b	60—d	78—c	96—d	114—b
7--a	25—b	43—c	61—b	79—a	97—c	115—a
8—d	26—b	44—b	62—b	80—a	98—c	116—b
9—d	27—b	45—c	63—b	81—c	99—b	117—c
10—c	28—c	46—a	64—a	82—b	100—c	118—a
11—b	29—d	47—c	65—b	83—d	101—c	119—d
12—c	30—c	48—a	66—b	84—c	102—c	
13—c	31—c	49—b	67—d	85—d	103—a	
14—c	32—c	50—c	68—d	86—a	104—a	
15—c	33—b	51—b	69—c	87—a	105—c	
16—c	34—b	52—b	70—d	88—b	106—b	
17—b	35—a	53—b	71—b	89—a	107—c	
18—b	36—b	54—c	72—a	90—b	108—a	

ELECTRICITY AND LIGHT THERAPY

1—d	6—d	11—b	16—c	21—c	26—d	31—b
2—a	7—b	12—d	17—b	22—b	27—c	32—b
3—a	8—c	13—c	18—c	23—a	28—d	33—d
4—b	9—d	14—d	19—d	24—d	29—d	34—d
5—b	10—a	15—b	20—a	25—b	30—b	

CHEMISTRY

1—a	8—d	15—d	22—b	29—a	36—b	43—d
2—b	9—a	16—a	23—b	30—a	37—b	44—b
3—d	10—b	17—d	24—d	31—d	38—c	45—b
4—a	11—c	18—a	25—d	32—b	39—a	46—c
5—a	12—c	19—c	26—c	33—b	40—a	47—c
6—a	13—c	20—a	27—c	34—c	41—c	48—a
7—c	14—a	21—c	28—c	35—c	42—c	49—c

THE SALON BUSINESS

1—d	12—b	23—a	34—c	45—a	56—c	67—c
2—a	13—c	24—a	35—a	46—c	57—b	68—b
3—d	14—d	25—c	36—a	47—b	58—b	69—a
4—b	15—a	26—d	37—b	48—c	59—d	70—b
5—b	16—c	27—b	38—c	49—b	60—b	
6—a	17—a	28—a	39—a	50—c	61—a	
7—c	18—b	29—b	40—a	51—a	62—c	
8—d	19—a	30—d	41—c	52—c	63—c	
9—a	20—c	31—a	42—d	53—d	64—d	
10—c	21—d	32—b	43—a	54—c	65—b	
11—b	22—b	33—d	44—b	55—d	66—a	

TEST 1

1—d	16—d	31—c	46—d	61—a	76—d	91—c
2—c	17—a	32—a	47—c	62—a	77—b	92—a
3—d	18—a	33—c	48—a	63—c	78—c	93—c
4—b	19—a	34—b	49—c	64—c	79—b	94—d
5—c	20—c	35—b	50—d	65—a	80—b	95—b
6—a	21—d	36—c	51—c	66—a	81—d	96—d
7—a	22—b	37—a	52—b	67—c	82—d	97—c
8—b	23—b	38—c	53—d	68—d	83—b	98—b
9—c	24—d	39—c	54—b	69—c	84—b	99—b
10—c	25—c	40—d	55—c	70—b	85—c	100—b
11—c	26—c	41—b	56—a	71—c	86—d	
12—d	27—c	42—d	57—c	72—d	87—c	
13—b	28—a	43—c	58—b	73—b	88—c	
14—a	29—c	44—a	59—c	74—b	89—a	
15—c	30—b	45—b	60—c	75—c	90—b	

6

TEST 2

1—b	16—b	31—a	46—d	61—c	76—b	91—b
2—c	17—b	32—d	47—b	62—a	77—d	92—c
3—a	18—a	33—a	48—b	63—b	78—d	93—c
4—d	19—d	34—b	49—b	64—a	79—b	94—a
5—c	20—d	35—a	50—c	65—b	80—b	95—d
6—c	21—d	36—d	51—c	66—d	81—d	96—b
7—d	22—b	37—c	52—b	67—c	82—b	97—a
8—b	23—d	38—a	53—d	68—c	83—a	98—b
9—c	24—a	39—b	54—b	69—d	84—a	99—a
10—c	25—c	40—b	55—c	70—a	85—c	100—b
11—d	26—b	41—d	56—c	71—d	86—a	
12—c	27—c	42—c	57—b	72—c	87—c	
13—b	28—c	43—b	58—a	73—d	88—a	
14—c	29—b	44—a	59—b	74—a	89—a	
15—c	30—b	45—c	60—c	75—b	90—b	